SACRAMENTAL TEACHING AND PRACTICE
IN THE REFORMATION CHURCHES

PATHWAY BOOKS

BIOGRAPHICAL NOTE

G. W BROMILEY, rector of St. Thomas' English Episcopal Church in Edinburgh, Scotland, is the author of a distinguished biography, *Thomas Cranmer: Reformer and Theologian,* a short introduction to Christian ethics, *Reasonable Service,* a study of baptism entitled, *Baptism and the Anglican Reformers,* and other books. He has contributed the article on "Authority of Scripture" in *The New Bible Commentary,* and he regularly writes articles and book reviews for theological journals. He is a Contributing Editor to *Christianity Today.* He holds the Ph.D. and D. Litt. degrees from the University of Edinburgh. From 1946 to 1951 he was lecturer and vice-principal at Tyndale Hall, Bristol.

Sacramental Teaching and Practice in the Reformation Churches

BY

G. W. BROMILEY, Ph.D., D. Litt.

Rector of St. Thomas' English Episcopal Church
Edinburgh, Scotland

WM. B. EERDMANS PUBLISHING COMPANY
GRAND RAPIDS, MICHIGAN

L. C. catalog card number: 57-14944
Printed in the United States of America
First printing, December 1957

ISBN 13: 978-0-8028-6330-0

CONTENTS

GENERAL INTRODUCTION

PATHWAY BOOKS are designed to help teachers, students, preachers, and laymen keep themselves informed on the important subjects and the crucial problems which confront the Christian church today. They are designed to help the reader bear witness to the Christian faith in the modern world.

Consulting Editors for Pathway Books are: F. F. Bruce, Head of the Department of Biblical History and Literature, University of Sheffield, England, and Editor of *The Evangelical Quarterly;* Leon Morris, Vice-Principal of Ridley College, Melbourne, Australia; Bernard Ramm, Director of Graduate Studies in Religion, Baylor University, Waco, Texas; and Edward J. Young, Professor of Old Testament, Westminster Theological Seminary, Philadelphia, Pennsylvania.

The writer of each volume is, of course, solely responsible for the opinions and judgments expressed in his book. The Consulting Editors give valuable suggestions and advice, but the choice of subject and author, and the general direction of the series is the responsibility of the publisher.

AUTHOR'S INTRODUCTION

IN THEIR FUNDAMENTAL NATURE and purpose the sacraments are extremely simple. They consist of short actions easily carried out and carrying an obvious meaning in themselves. They were instituted to help our understanding of the Gospel, to induce or strengthen our faith in Jesus Christ and to further our obedience and discipleship. Their very simplicity as concrete actions is a mark of the gracious condescension of God to our human weakness, the signs giving vividness and power where words alone might seem remote, or speaking with their own eloquence where the spoken message is not readily understood.

Because they are so simple in essence, we might suppose that the sacraments would not give rise to any great problems of practice or theology. But in fact this has not been the case. Perhaps it is because the simplicity is the kind which carries with it great profundity rather than mere superficiality, but the fact remains that some of the greatest battles have been and are being fought over sacramental administration and understanding. Indeed, the more we study the matter, the more we see that these simple signs instituted and used by God involve depths which cannot easily be plumbed and thus give rise to problems which are not easily solved.

There are those, for example, who are wiser than God and do not see why we should have sacraments at all, or who depreciate them almost to the point of non-observance. These persons stand for the thing signified, for the baptism of the Holy Spirit or nourishment by living fellowship with Jesus Christ, but they see in the external signs something which is at best superfluous and at worst a definite stumbling-block.

Again, differences arise as to the details of administration. The basic action necessarily remains more or less the same, but all kinds of variations are possible within the common structure. Washing with water may take the form of immersion, effusion, or even sprinkling, and it may or may not be

7

accompanied by other acts or ceremonies. Bread and wine can be taken in many different forms and attitudes, and again the simple act of eating and drinking can be set against a varied liturgical background. How far the different forms and accompaniments are legitimate and helpful is a question which calls for careful consideration and can give rise to many sincere differences of opinion — even among those who accept a common norm in Holy Scripture.

More seriously, there are the divergent interpretations of the sacraments which have occasioned so much bitter strife through the centuries of Christian history. Some of the disputes are almost questions of administration, as for example the question whether baptism should be given the children of professing Christians, but they have theological implications which give them a more serious aspect. The actual meaning of the sacraments has not caused such serious division, though there have of course been differences of emphasis and deficiencies in understanding. But when it comes to the operations of the sacraments, their effects, their mode of working, and their relationship to the work of Jesus Christ and the Holy Spirit, the most divergent doctrines have been taught, and the giving of an official dogmatic status to some of the suggestions made has embittered the whole discussion, frustrating any real effort at mutual enrichment and correction. Indeed, were it not that all parties begin at a common point, and owe some kind of allegiance to the one scriptural norm, it might seem that the paths have diverged so widely that there can be little hope of any *rapprochement*. In fact, however, the common elements remain even under what seem to be the most distorted forms, and by way of a genuine biblical understanding it may be that the churches can find common ground again in their theology, as also in their administration, of the sacraments.

In the present study we shall be primarily concerned with sacramental practice and interpretation as they are to be found in the Reformation churches and more especially those which took the Reformed rather than the Lutheran path. But this does not mean that we shall be committed merely to an historical survey. The main interest of the Reformers themselves was to be true to the teaching of Holy Scripture itself, and we shall be most loyal to them if, along the general lines of their tradition, we attempt a biblical rather than an historical statement. This will have a threefold advantage. It will submit the Reformed interpretation itself to its own biblical standard. It will bring us into fruitful contact with other views in which over-emphases or distortions conceal positive elements of truth. And it will give to our discussion a living relevance for Christians of the present day, for whom the sacraments may never be regarded merely as objects of scientific inquiry, but must always be gratefully used as divinely ordained means of blessing.

CHAPTER ONE

THE TWO SACRAMENTS

A FIRST QUESTION which arises is what is meant by a sacrament, what ceremonies are to be accepted as sacraments, and whether the sacraments can be brought under a common sacramental theology or must be treated independently. To many people brought up exclusively in a particular tradition it may seem that these matters are self-evident. But a little thought will show that we have problems here which cannot be avoided and different answers which can have very serious results in sacramental practice and understanding.

The root of the trouble is that the term *sacrament* is not itself a biblical word, and indeed, that the Bible does not give us any term for the ordinances in question. The word *mystery* was often used in the early church, and this had the advantage of being a scriptural term,[1] although it does not seem to be applied specifically to the sacraments. *Sacrament* itself is a Latin term for the oath engaging a soldier to obedience, and merely describes an aspect of what is involved in these means of grace. By custom it has naturally come to have a more specialized and more comprehensive significance, being applied to a divine act which carries with it a specific meaning or grace. But the fact remains that we use for these ordinances a word which is not itself scriptural, and thus there is always the danger that its use may be controlled by theology or practice rather than by the Bible itself. Indeed, many of the controversies concerning the sacraments in general are due to looseness in the understanding of this term, and might well have been avoided if care had been taken to subject it to biblical control.

1. E.g., Eph. 3:3, I Tim. 3:16.

It might be argued that, since the term is not biblical, it is better to avoid it altogether. On the other hand, it must be remembered that the Bible itself does not give us any alternative, so that if actions like baptism and the Lord's Supper are in any way related, and may rightly be considered together, it is surely permissible to use some such word. The only thing is that we have to be sure to give it a scriptural reference rather than merely give it a vague and loose definition, or feed into it our own conception of what a sacrament might or ought to be.

The Reformers found it necessary to make a correction at this point in face of the opinion and practice current in their own day. After a period of confusion, when the word *sacrament* had been applied generally to all kinds of signs or actions with a certain spiritual significance, the church in the West had come to use it of seven ceremonies in a more precise and specialized sense. Now it has always been admitted that we may give to the word a more extended meaning in which it may cover all the material things which speak to us of God and His actions, so that ultimately the universe itself may be regarded as sacramental by the Christian. For do not the visible things of God speak of the things that are invisible? But it is rather another matter to bring the particular signs of the Gospel in the New Testament under the category of these more general sacraments, interpreting the former in terms of the latter. And it is a different matter again when a particular definition of sacraments is adopted which allows the bringing together of such diverse ceremonies (all biblical in their own way) as baptism, ordination, marriage, and unction.

The point is that when we turn to the Bible we find that the two actions of baptism and the Lord's Supper have features which cannot be attributed to any others, as even the champions of seven sacraments are forced to admit when they speak of the pre-eminence of the first two. To begin with, it is evident that these two sacraments are directly instituted by the Lord Himself, not only by His own example in submitting to baptism[2] and taking part in the first communion,[3] but also by His express command to the apostles

2. Matt. 3:13.
3. Matt. 26:26.

both to baptize[4] and to "do this."[5] But the same cannot easily be said of confirmation or penance, for example, whatever scriptural justification may be sought for these practices on other grounds.

Again, these two sacraments stand in close relation to the saving work of Jesus Christ in a way which cannot be said of any other observances that may be termed sacramental in a loose and extended sense. For Jesus Christ Himself calls His cross and passion both a baptism and a cup,[6] the bread of the Supper being also linked directly with His body, broken in self-offering. Marriage and ordination may in their own ways be related to the reconciling acts of God, or may reflect the relationship between Christ and His people, but they do not stand in the same direct connection to the heart of Christ's atoning work in His death and passion.

This connection of baptism and the Lord's Supper with the saving action of Christ does not consist only in the fact that Jesus calls His death a baptism and a cup, and institutes them within the context of His reconciling work. For in these two cases, unlike other observances, the actions themselves reflect and therefore bear witness to the work which Jesus Christ accomplished. Baptism is essentially an enactment of death and resurrection, and the breaking of the bread and outpouring of the wine is for the life and nourishment of others. By their very character, therefore, these two sacraments stand in a category by themselves, and cannot simply be classified with other ecclesiastical ceremonies.

The close relationship between these signs and the atoning work of Jesus Christ means that they form in themselves a witness to this work, and therefore carry with them the promise of forgiveness and new life[7] which is the very essence of the Christian message. Many actions may have a spiritual significance and yet not be linked with the basis of the evangel. But the sacraments ordained by the Lord are in a very real sense sacraments of the Gospel, used by the Holy Spirit to bring home to us the gracious benefits of God in

4. Luke 22:19.
5. Matt. 28:19.
6. Matt. 20:22.
7. Cf. Acts 2:38.

Jesus Christ, and therefore have an integral place in the whole of God's work towards us and in us.

But this leads us to the further point that baptism and the Lord's Supper are connected in a special sense with the preaching of the Gospel. This is explicitly the case with baptism, for the baptismal command in Matthew 28 links it with the making of disciples and the teaching of the things commanded by the Lord.[8] But in essence it is no less true of the Lord's Supper, which at its institution was set in the last discourses of the Lord to His disciples, and the accompanying word of which is itself a short proclamation of the Gospel. Indeed, the actions themselves have often been described as the visible word of the Gospel, in virtue of their character, so that it is essential to them to be related to the audible word of proclamation.

A further distinctive feature of these two signs as compared with other meaningful ceremonies is that they correspond to the two great covenantal signs of the Old Testament, circumcision[9] and the passover.[10] In the Old Testament and among the Jews there were, of course, many other ceremonies, and some of these, as we can see from the Epistle to the Hebrews, had a very real significance in relation to the atoning work of Jesus Christ. But circumcision and the passover occupied a peculiar place as the two great covenantal signs, and it is instructive that they find their continuance in the two analogous but bloodless signs which are the pre-eminent sacraments of the New Testament.

In view of the fact that there are so many important peculiarities, it is essential that in our terminology we should make a clear distinction between these two signs and other ceremonies which may be useful and significant but obviously do not have the same character. It is for this reason that the Reformation churches reserve the term sacrament for baptism and the Lord's Supper. In so doing, they do not condemn or discontinue the proper use of other ceremonies. Ordination, for example, has its own place in the church.[11] A form of confirmation is necessary where the children of professing

8. Matt. 28:19.
9. Cf. Col. 2:11,12.
10. Cf. Matt. 26:17ff.
11. Acts 14:23.

Christians are baptized in infancy.[12] Marriage, too, is something which has a special meaning in the case of Christians since it reflects the spiritual marriage and union between Christ and the church.[13] But the fact remains that even though a deep significance may be seen in these and many other actions, they are not actions which belong to the same category as those instituted by Christ and so evidently related to His saving work and its proclamation. Hence it is better that the term sacrament, if it is to be used at all, should be restricted to these dominical or evangelical sacraments, and some other term used for other significant ceremonies, actions, or processes. Alternatively, a new word might be coined for baptism and the Lord's Supper and *sacrament* merely used in a loose and general sense. But in view of the centuries of usage already behind us this would give rise to more difficulties than it would solve.

The distinction between the two evangelical sacraments and other signs is clear to see, but the question remains whether there are sufficient similarities between the two to bring them under a common term and to give us a general sacramental theology. In some quarters it has been suggested that baptism and the Lord's Supper are distinct signs and therefore must be interpreted individually rather than in terms of one another. In some sense, this was the contention of traditionalists in the 16th century, who placed the Holy Communion in a class by itself, finding in it certain special features of divine presence and action which could not be seen or stated in relation to baptism. But it might also seem to be a biblical procedure since the Bible does not find a common term for the two or treat them together. Even though we are right to isolate these two actions, are we justified in considering them together as the two sacraments of the Gospel?

The answer seems to be given by the important features which we have already found to be common to them in contradistinction to other rites which are merely sacramental in a very loose and general sense. If these were merely small and insignificant points, then we might agree that although these actions are marked off from others they have nothing material

12. Rom. 10:9.
13. Eph. 5:25ff.

in common and there can be no such thing as a genuine
sacramental theology. In fact, however, the common features
are all of such importance that they not only justify us in
finding a general term for the two actions but provide us
with the elements of a common theology. Though the Bible
does not give us a word, it gives us the thing itself for which
a word must be found and for which the customary term
sacrament may be used for want of a better. And in virtue of
these special features, there are many things which have to
be said of both actions as well as those which have to be said
of each in particular.

For one thing, the fact that a sacrament in the true sense
is an action specifically ordained by God Himself invites
reflection on its purpose in the divine economy. Within the
ministry of the Gospel, God has appointed that there should
be works as well as words. This is a condescension to our
weakness, as the Reformers see. It is easier for us to appre-
hend something seen and done than something which is
merely said. But there is something deeper to it than this.
For the whole of God's saving work is an action as well as a
verbal revelation. The Word was made flesh.[14] Salvation was
not merely declared, but achieved. God worked out His purposes in terms of a human life and death and resurrection.
In the days of His flesh Jesus Christ acted as well as taught.[15]
And when the Gospel is preached, this fact finds its reflection
in sacramental action. Once again we have to do with an
enacted as well as a spoken word.

But this being the case, it is essential that the sacrament
should stand in a firm and clear relationship to the work of
Jesus Christ. In a sense, all actions in the church are related
to the basis of the whole life and activity of Christians in
what was done by the Lord. But in many cases the connection is only loose and indirect. In the case of a sacrament,
however, the whole meaning and power of the action are
not to be found in the action itself, but in the action which
it reflects. Indeed, we might put it even more strongly. The
real sacrament is the meaningful action of God in Jesus
Christ — the true baptism and the true cup.[16] And the signs

14. John 1:14.
15. Cf. John 5:17.
16. Matt. 20:22.

which we call sacraments have meaning and power only insofar as and because they are in their own way the declaration of this basic action.

They can be this declaration, however, only insofar as they carry their meaning discernibly within themselves. The sacrament must be not merely a meaningful sign. It must be a sign with a particular meaning. It must be an enacted and visible Gospel. It may be so in different ways and with different emphases, as the two very different actions of baptism and the Lord's Supper show. But as a "visible word" (Augustine) a sacrament must be of such a nature as to declare the Gospel with which it is indissolubly linked.

But the indissoluble relationship with the Gospel carries with it an equally indissoluble relationship with the evangelical word. The action cannot stand alone, just as the mere act of the crucifixion has no relevance apart from its meaning — that God was in Christ reconciling the world to Himself.[17] This relationship is safeguarded against final dissolution by the inclusion of a sacramental word in the very action. As Augustine said, it is only when the word is added that we have a sacrament. But the mere formula of institution is in itself an inadequate proclamation of the word. It is essential that the sacramental action should in all practicable circumstances be accompanied by a definite proclamation of the Gospel, so that the word is heard as well as seen, the action confirming the declaration and the declaration explaining the action.

In this connection, the Reformation churches feel it necessary to maintain that the sacrament should not only be accompanied by the word, but should be subordinate to it. This does not mean that the sacrament is unimportant or superfluous. But it means that it is secondary whereas the word is primary. There can be word without sacrament, but there cannot be sacrament without word. And normally the word initiates and the sacrament confirms. The obvious reason for this order is that the sacraments are so plainly secondary in the institution and action of the New Testament apostolate, or for that matter, in the practice of Jesus Himself. The spoken word is the primary instrument chosen and used by God for the declaring of the Gospel and the calling

17. II Cor. 5:19.

of men to faith and discipleship. More deeply, we are reminded that the true sacramental action declared is the once-for-all life and death and resurrection of Jesus Christ which the baptismal and eucharistic action can only reflect. More deeply still, the order is a witness that the saving action of God on earth is a fulfillment of the determinate will and counsel of God from eternity, and that if our salvation was effected in and by the incarnation, it was the Word which was made flesh. The order is not, then, incidental or capricious, but one which is grounded in the whole work of God, and ultimately in God Himself.

The relationship of the sacrament with the word is a reminder that this witness to the Gospel cannot be considered apart from the work of the Holy Spirit. Even in the New Testament, baptism in particular is brought into close relationship with the Spirit. We read of the Holy Spirit descending upon Christ at His own baptism in Jordan.[18] We read of the promised baptism with the Holy Ghost and with fire.[19] In John 3 we read of the need to be born again of water and of the Holy Ghost.[20] In the case of Cornelius we read that the descent of the Spirit is regarded as a compelling reason for baptism with water.[21] The same direct relationship is not seen so plainly in regard to Holy Communion, but the Bible leaves us in no doubt that the whole work of witness to Jesus Christ by word and sacrament is an operation in which the Holy Spirit must play a leading role. For He it is supremely whose office it is to bear witness to the Lord.[22] This does not mean, of course, that there is a necessary, automatic, or static connection between the outward administration either of the word or a sacramental rite and the ministry of the Spirit. But it does mean that the sacraments, like the word, are means by which the Holy Spirit is at work. It means that they must be administered with prayer to the Spirit. It means that their ultimate efficacy depends upon the sovereign decision and action of the Spirit. It means that their real work, brought to fruition in God's

18. Matt. 3:16.
19. Matt. 3:11; Acts 1:5.
20. John 3:5.
21. Acts 10:47.
22. John 15:26.

good time, is the genuine, inward work of regeneration manifested in repentance and faith, mortification and renewal, abiding and increase in Jesus Christ.

There is just one final point. The sacraments are at one in that they both involve recipients. As we shall have cause to notice, there is a difference in the mode of reception. But as in baptism there is not only a washing and one who washes, but a person washed, so in the Lord's Supper there is not only a feeding and a dispenser of bread and wine, but one who partakes. This is important, for it means that the individual is caught up, as it were, into the action instituted and used by God, and has his own secondary but necessary place within it. This individual to whom the sacrament applies is the man who makes the response of repentance and faith, to which he is summoned by the sacrament and the evoking or strengthening of which is itself the work of the sacrament. To be sure, the supreme thing about the sacraments is that they are the means of the grace of God. But the fact that I am the recipient underlines the fact that the grace of God is for me and that I must accept it. Hence, while the sacraments witness to the objective fact that Jesus Christ has died, the one for the many,[23] they are used by the Holy Spirit in the bringing home of this objective fact to the many for whom He has died.

In sum, while the two dominical or evangelical sacraments are not merely repetitive, but have individual features and emphases, there are significant common elements which make it possible for us to speak of a sacramental theology and to compare them with one another and with the word to which they are closely related. Instituted by the one Lord for one general purpose, they have their part in the witness to the saving work of Jesus Christ, and therefore in the operation of the Holy Spirit applying this work in and to believers. It is in this context, and along these lines, that they are to be understood and used in the church.

23. Rom. 5:12ff.

CHAPTER TWO

HOLY BAPTISM

———————

HOLY BAPTISM as it is known from the New Testament and practiced in the church is the sacrament of washing with water in the name of the Trinity.[1] It is the first of the two sacraments, administered once only at the point of initiation into the Christian community. As we shall notice later, the details of administration vary, but the essential action and the accompanying words are constant factors where Christian baptism is given.

Various derivations have been suggested for the rite. Washings have been practiced in many religions, and figure in the Old Testament, being also used by Jewish sects. But there can be no doubt that Christian baptism has its origin with the baptism of John, and especially with the baptism of Jesus by John,[2] and the taking up of baptism by Jesus and His disciples. Thus we are told in John's Gospel that even during the Lord's ministry the disciples practiced baptism,[3] and Matthew of course gives us the direct command of the risen Christ that His apostles should baptize as well as preach and teach.[4]

Yet in the New Testament a new and significant factor appears in relation to baptism. For it is not just a washing — even as a sign of repentance or a confession of faith. A special word is used for baptism which marks it off from the religious lustrations common in other faiths. Christian baptism is a new thing, covering far more than the mere rite of washing.

1. Matt. 28:19.
2. Matt. 3:13ff.; Mark 1:9ff.; Luke 3:21ff.; John 1:29ff.
3. John 4:1.
4. Matt. 28:19.

In its full sense, it brings us to the very core of our salvation in the work of Christ. The Reformers emphasize the point by claiming that strictly baptism is the thing signified as well as the sign, and by finding the thing signified, not in what we do, but in what God does for us.

The clue to the meaning of baptism is to be found in the baptism of Jesus Himself at the hands of John.[5] As was noted by many sixteenth-century exegetes, all the persons of the Trinity are present and active at this baptism. The Father speaks the word of election from heaven, acknowledging Jesus as the elected Son. Baptism is thus a sacrament of the covenant of election. The Son is the One baptized, accepting the baptism of repentance, and thus entering the way of identification with sinners which was to reach its climax in His obedient self-offering on the cross.[6] Baptism is thus a sacrament of the fulfillment of the covenant in the substitutionary death and resurrection of the incarnate Son. The Holy Spirit is the One who descends upon the Son, empowering Him for the ministry upon which He enters.[7] Baptism is thus a sacrament of the outpouring of the Holy Ghost.

The decisive link, it will be seen, is with the saving action of the Son in His obedient life, its climax upon the cross, and its culmination in His resurrection. In this respect the Lord's description of His death as a baptism is all-important.[8] Many exegetes have missed the significance of this statement, as though what we have here were merely an incidental comparison. But far from being incidental, it brings us to the very heart of the matter. The saving work of Jesus Christ is the real baptism, the accomplished baptismal work, and the rite itself is the witness and reflection which stands in inseparable connection with it. Unless this point is grasped, our whole understanding of baptism will inevitably be distorted, insoluble problems will be introduced, and the result will be all kinds of errors and confusion.

When baptism is administered, the recipient is not merely making a confession of his own repentance and faith, and witnessing to something which takes place in himself. He is

5. Matt. 3:14.
6. Matt. 3:15.
7. Matt. 3:16.
8. Luke 12:50; Matt. 20:22.

baptized into the name of the Trinity, and therefore into the saving action of the Trinity on his behalf. His baptism speaks to him, therefore, of the election of the Father which is the ground and basis of his salvation. The beginning is not to be sought in a decision which he makes, but in a prior decision which God has already made, and which alone makes possible his decision. To make baptism supremely an expression of the believer's own choice of God is a common mistake which is easily made where there is an evangelistic concern, but which the Reformers with their scriptural understanding are careful to avoid.

Attesting this eternal election, baptism speaks to the believer of its fulfillment in the substitutionary work of the Son. He rests upon a finished work to which he need not and cannot add anything. Not even by his repentance and faith can he do anything for himself. That is why baptism can be, as it was to Luther, a sign which gives confidence in times of temptation, doubt, or actual backsliding. It does not remind him merely of his own past experience, nor does it merely assure him that a sacramental action has been performed, but it takes him to the finished substitutionary work of Jesus Christ, and therefore to the sole but sufficient ground of forgiveness and acceptance.

Finally, as an attestation of the election fulfilled in Jesus Christ, baptism speaks to him of the work of the Holy Spirit by which he is caught up into the action of Jesus Christ. Not only did Jesus Christ Himself teach and act and die and rise again in the power of the Holy Spirit, but the Holy Spirit does the work of incorporation into the life and death and resurrection of Jesus Christ, so graphically depicted in the baptismal action. Even here, where it is a matter of the believer's being called and claimed for the new life effected in Christ, there is no question of baptism being a witness to anything that he himself initiates or does. It is primarily to the sovereign action of the Holy Spirit who, like the wind, blows where He lists,[9] but upon whose action he can count where there is prayer and the faithful preaching of the word of the cross.

The fact that there is this appropriation to the work of Jesus Christ means, of course, that there is a definite accept-

9. John 3:8.

ance and reflection of the death and resurrection of Jesus Christ in the believer. That is why there has always been the insistence upon some confession of repentance and faith, either by the adult convert, by the Christian parent presenting his child, or by the sponsor in the name or on behalf of the child. Baptism comes to us with the reminder, which is also the summons, that the work of the Holy Spirit, in relation to the election of the Father and the substitution of the Son, means the genuine end of our old life and beginning of the new, and that this will find acceptance and confession in the movement of self-denial and renewal, of repentance, faith, and obedience.[10]

Where baptism is administered to the children of professing Christians, it will carry with it from the very outset the call to enter into the saving work which has been done once and for all upon the cross. The baptized is to accept the real fact attested to him by baptism that in Christ his sinful life is judged and put away, and the acceptance of this fact means repentance, the denial of this old life of sin, and the readiness to acknowledge it justly condemned and crucified. But equally he is to accept the real fact attested to him by baptism that in Christ his new and eternal life has begun, and acceptance of this fact means faith, the affirmation of this new life of righteousness, the readiness to acknowledge it as his new and true life before God and therefore in fact. It will not be forgotten that repentance and faith are themselves possible only in the Holy Spirit and not merely as a human reaction. Nor will it be forgotten that they may come in many different ways, sometimes by a steady and almost imperceptible process, sometimes in a more striking or even drastic crisis. But either way, baptism calls for this first step in correspondence with the divine work of death and resurrection which it declares.

Where baptism is administered to a convert in whom there has already been the first acceptance in repentance and faith of the end of the old life and beginning of the new, it will be to him a witness and assurance that the death and resurrection into which he has entered are an objective reality. He will be taught not to rest in himself, in his own experience or emotions or beliefs, but in the finished work into

10. Rom. 6:3ff.

which he is incorporated when he accepts the denial of self in repentance and the renewal of self in faith. And he will remember that even his acceptance is not something on which he can pride himself as though it were primarily his own choice or achievement. For only in the Holy Spirit, and in response to the word of the cross, can there be any genuine repentance and faith.

Nor is the message of baptism exhausted by the summons to repentance and faith, or the assurance that the real work of Jesus Christ rests behind repentance and faith and gives it meaning and substance. However baptism is administered, whether to children or those professing conversion, it carries with it also a call to the working out of the new reality in Christ in a life of discipleship and obedience. If Jesus Christ has died and risen again for us and in our place, so that we are dead with Him and the life which we now live is our life in Christ, it is not enough merely to accept this fact in an initial act of repentance and faith. This new and true reality must be accepted and worked out in a life of mortification and renewal which reflects and corresponds to the death and resurrection of Christ. Thus baptism is a summons which is with the Christian throughout his life. It is not just an ethical call It is a summons to be what we really are, to live our new and true life. It is an imperative based on, and drawing its power and authority from, an indicative. We are dead, and our life is hid with Christ in God.[11] Therefore, we are not to seek the things on earth, but the things which are above.

The Reformers from Luther onwards worked out this theme with great vigor, particularly in relation to the mortification of the old life. Baptism challenges us to a real drowning of the old self. Not only must the ways and habits and thoughts of the old self-centered sinner be put off, but the very man of sin himself.[12] Nor is this a task easily accomplished in some great crisis. It may have critical points, but it is a work which will go on as long as we are on earth, and the more we do in fact bring our desires and appetites and opinions and actions under the cross the more we shall see how deeply the call of baptism cuts. Yet we shall not be

11. Col. 3:3.
12. Eph. 4:22, Col. 3:5.

despondent, for we know that this is merely a bringing of our life into conformity with its new being in Christ.[13] Even as a summons baptism is still a witness. The old man is dead indeed, crucified once and for all on the cross of Golgotha.[14] If the work of mortification is long and arduous, if the old man clings to his shadowy life and is loath to die, the victory is already won. In the power of the cross, through the means of grace in the judging word, the witnessing sacrament, convicting prayer and chastening abstinence, real progress can be made in this essential process.

But the Christian life is not merely or primarily negative. Christ did not die just to destroy sin, but to give new life. Hence, baptism calls us not only to the abandonment of the old life from which we are now freed because it is ended, but to the enjoyment and exercise of the new life into which we are initiated as it is begun in and with the resurrection of Jesus Christ.[15] If there has to be mortification, there has also to be vivification. If there has to be criticism, there has also to be construction. If the old has to be put off, the new has to be put on. New opinions have to be learned, new ways of thought adopted, new habits formed, new modes of speech and action accepted, new associations entered into, new aims and purposes seen, new service rendered. As Paul puts it, the man in Christ is a new creature, and all things are made new.[16] This is literally true. Hence there need be no despondency if the process is slow and difficult. Jesus Christ is risen from the dead. The life in Him is our true life.[17] The summons of baptism is again the witness to the true reality. And in the power of the resurrection, and through the means of grace in the life-giving word, the encouraging sacrament, inspiriting prayer and edifying exercises, there can be a genuine manifestation of the positive fruits of the Spirit, in life, fellowship, and service.

Baptism as the sign of death and resurrection is a witness and a summons, pointing us to the work of salvation accomplished on our behalf in Jesus Christ, and calling us to accept

13. Rom. 12:2, Phil. 2:5ff.
14. Rom. 6:6, Gal. 2:20, Col. 3:3,9.
15. Eph. 4:24.
16. II Cor. 5:17.
17. Col. 3:4,10.

this new reality by repentance and faith, mortification and renewal. But it is also a promise, assuring us of the consummation of our redemption in dissolution and resurrection, when the old man loses the last vestiges of his life and the new man is manifested in his truth and fullness. Thus baptism is a sacrament which remains with the Christian to the end of his life on earth. By its very witness to the finished work of Christ, and as a call to action upon this basis, it has for him an ultimate assurance even when he comes to his last hour. The day of death is a day when the crucifixion of the old man receives its definitive answer and acceptance, when even its unreal life is concluded, when the believer is literally put to death with Christ as Christ was put to death for him.[18]

In this connection baptism sheds an illuminating light on the mysteries of suffering and death, as Luther so finely saw. It shows us that these are not things which have escaped the beneficent providence of God, although at first it might appear that this is the case. On the contrary, even death itself is taken and used as an instrument of good. This would be true in a general sense even apart from the work of Christ, for death as the consequence and penalty of sin[19] is a means to contain and destroy sin. But when we come to the cross we see that this is so in a deeper and more particular sense. By submitting to death on behalf of sinners, the sinless Lamb of God overcame death, making it not merely an instrument of preservation, but of salvation.[20] And as it is by the denial of self in repentance and mortification that the believer accepts the substitutionary death of Christ, ceasing to be the old sinner, so it is by the denial of self in literal dissolution that this acceptance is worked out and the reality now known by faith is consummated. But the light shed on death is also in some sense a light on suffering too. For not only are the sufferings of this present time beneath comparison with the glory to be revealed,[21] but they help forward the work of mortification, showing us that it is a real thing, teaching us not to put our trust in that which belongs to the old life,

18. This is perhaps the meaning of I Cor. 15:29.
19. Rom. 6:23.
20. I Pet. 2:24.
21. Rom. 8:18.

reminding us that the old life is in any case a life without a future, and summoning us therefore to accept the reality of our crucifixion and resurrection in Jesus Christ.

But baptism does not merely reassure us that even death has been appropriated and used by our saving God. It also holds before us the promise of our resurrection with Jesus Christ when we shall enter into the fullness of the new life which is ours in virtue of His resurrection.[22] Already this new life is our true life.[23] For the moment, however, although we accept it in faith and express it in renewal, it is a life of faith and not of sight.[24] Only Jesus Christ, the first-fruits, has entered into its fullness, the One for the many. But in baptism we have the promise that this resurrection life in and with Jesus Christ is for us, too, so that in the declining years of life and at the time of death baptism comes to its final splendor as a sign, not of empty yearning, but of the sure and certain hope grounded upon its witness to the death and resurrection of Jesus Christ. Only with this final entry into Christ's work, and in correspondence with it, does the sign cease to carry a message for us, and it does so only because we are then caught up fully into the thing signified, the true reality of baptism, the work of the triune God on our behalf.

Although baptism thus has a reference to the whole life of the Christian, unlike the second sacrament it is administered only once.[25] This point has so impressed itself upon Christendom from an early age that the majority of churches, however exclusive in other respects, are prepared to acknowledge the baptism of others so long as they are satisfied that it is administered with water and in the name of the Trinity. The practice of a single administration derives, of course, from New Testament days, but important theological reasons have been seen for the practice. Baptism is the initiatory sign, and for that reason alone it should not be repeated. It is the sign of regeneration, and although there may be many restorations, birth can take place only once. Supremely, however, it is the sign of the work of Jesus Christ which emphasizes the once-for-all character of this work. Unlike the high-priests of

22. Rom. 6:5.
23. Gal. 2:20.
24. II Cor. 5:7.
25. Eph. 4:5.

the Old Testament, Jesus did not have to make His offering many times, nor does it need to be repeated. He offered Himself once for the sins of the world.[26] And the one baptism for the remission of sins attests the uniqueness of this offering. It was thus a serious error, as we shall see later, that a kind of repetition of baptism was found in the so-called sacrament of penance. And although their own convictions did not allow them to see it in this light, Anabaptists caused a great shock to the 16th century Reformers by presuming to repeat the one sacrament of the once-for-all death and resurrection of Christ.

As a sign which is administered once only, and the administration of which is quite generally accepted, even in different churches, baptism is in a very real sense a sacrament of Christian unity. This is the case practically, for those who are baptized even with what is regarded as heretical baptism are marked off as Christians from the world of the non-baptized. But even more so is it the case theologically. For it points us to the basis and the reality of the unity of believers in the one work of Jesus Christ. As the true baptism is His substitutionary death and resurrection once for all, so we are all baptized into the one Christ. Our separate lives of sin come to an end. Even they too in their death are united in the crucified body of Jesus Christ.[27] And we do not have a series of individual new lives, but the resurrection life of Jesus Christ is the life of all.[28] Bringing us to the central point on which the old converges and from which the new radiates, the one baptism speaks to us of the indestructible unity of believers which persists in spite of their disunities, and which they are to accept and express as they accept as the true reality their life in Jesus Christ. That which unites is not the external sign. It is the thing signified. But the external sign, once administered, is a powerful witness to this inescapable unity, a summons to give it expression in personal and ecclesiastical relationships, and a promise of its final realization in the resurrection life of eternity.

Thus far we have spoken of baptism mainly in terms of its meaning. And the Reformers, taught by Scripture, saw that

26. Heb. 9:26ff.
27. II Cor. 5:14.
28. II Cor. 5:15.

there can be no isolation of the sign from its meaning. But it has always been realized that baptism, like the word of God, is more than an eloquent action. It is also an effective action. It does not merely attest the grace of God. It is itself, in the Holy Spirit, a means of grace. If it can be called a sign, it must also be called an effective sign, something which God has instituted in order that He may achieve certain results through it.[29] But to speak of baptism as an operative or effective sign raises certain problems which, if they cannot be fully solved, do at least call for a certain amount of discussion. How does the sacrament achieve its effect? In what circumstances and in what degree is the effect to be expected? What is indeed the effect to which we refer? At a later point we must give brief consideration to mistaken views on this point which we must be careful to understand and avoid. For the moment, however, a more positive statement may be attempted.

In the first place, we have to realize that the real work of baptism, that which is not merely attested but effected in baptism, is a finished work. This has nothing whatever to do with the so-called *ex opere operato* view of baptismal efficacy. It has nothing whatever to do with a work done in us at all, but with a work done for us, in our place. As the true baptism is the saving work of Jesus Christ, so the true work of baptism is the substitutionary death and resurrection effected in Him on behalf of the many.[30] Naturally, the external administration of the rite cannot do this work. It cannot add to it or repeat it. But the fact remains that it is an effected work. It is something which has been done, and can neither be done again nor undone. It has something which has been genuinely done, more solidly and validly and definitively than any response that can ever take place in us. We cannot crucify ourselves with Christ; we are crucified in and with Him.[31] Nor can we raise ourselves again with Christ; we are raised in and with Him.[32] If baptism attests to us the saving action of God in Christ, it is an effective sign first and last and all the time because that which it attests has been really

29. Cf. Rom. 6:4.
30. II Cor. 5:14.
31. Gal. 2:20.
32. Col. 3:1.

done. And any discussion of the effects of baptism which fails
not merely to presuppose but to emphasize this finished work
is bound to lead to serious misunderstanding.

Yet this is not the end of the matter. For if baptism tells
us, like the word, that we are dead in Christ and therefore
forgiven, that we are also raised with Him and therefore
regenerated, it is also a means under the Holy Spirit to bring
about or to further the acceptance of this reality in the
response of repentance and faith, mortification and renewal.
It may do this in different ways in different cases. As we have
seen already, in those baptized in infancy and thus brought
under the sphere of the Gospel, it may be a means to bring
about the first acceptance. In all cases, it can seal this response. In all cases again, it can be a summons to the
furtherance of the subjective answer. But whatever the individual circumstances, there are certain basic points which
demand our attention.

First, there can be no question of an effecting of the primary work of remission and regeneration, as though this had
to take place in us before it could have any genuine truth
or validity. It is surprising how often the full bearing and
reality of substitution are overlooked in this connection, even
by those who maintain it formally. To be sure, there is a
secondary work of repentance and regeneration in us, the
acceptance of Christ and His work, the entry into or identification with or response to Him in repentance and faith,
mortification and renewal. But the fact remains that in the
One who died and rose again for the many[33] our death for
sin and resurrection for justification have taken place once
and for all. Anything else which takes place can do so only
on the basis and in the strength of this finished work on our
behalf and in our stead.

Second, the operation of the sacrament in the evoking or
furtherance of our movement of response can take place only
under the sovereign disposal of the Holy Spirit whose office
it is to initiate and control this movement. This involves a
qualification. It is a dangerous thing to take the Holy Spirit
for granted, however correctly or punctiliously we may obey
the command to baptize.[34] As already stated, there must be

33. II Cor. 5:14,15.
34. John 3:8.

prayer for the Holy Spirit. On the other hand, it removes all qualifications. For nothing is too hard for the Lord. The subjects of baptism may not be very promising ones. They may even be infants in whom it seems that there can be no response. But we are not just in the sphere of natural or psychological possibilities. We are not to say with Mary and Nicodemus: "How can these things be?"[35] We are in the sphere of the life-giving Spirit, and therefore, against all human hope,[36] we can administer the sacrament with hope of its fruitful operation if we do so in humble and prayerful dependence on the Holy Ghost.

Third, the work of baptism, like that of the sacraments generally, stands in strict relationship to the meaning, and therefore to the evangelical word of which it is the visible form. Much of the misunderstanding of its operation is due to the attempted isolation of the effect from the meaning and therefore from the word, as though the action itself had some quasi-magical power. The whole point is that baptism, rightly conjoined with the Gospel, points us to the work already done for us in Christ, and summons and impells us in the Holy Spirit to accept this work, and thus to make the responsive movement of repentance and faith, mortification and renewal. It is not the external administration which effects anything in itself, but the meaningful sacrament of the saving action of Christ as this is linked with the word and applied and used by the Holy Ghost.

This has certain important implications for our understanding of the work, or rather of the outworking, of baptism in our own lives. In the first place, baptism, like Christ Himself, must be perceived and received as both the action of man and the action of God. In this respect the sacrament reflects the incarnation of Jesus Christ, very God and very man. And as it is tragically possible to see in Jesus Christ only a great religious teacher and example, and therefore to miss His true significance, so it is possible to receive baptism merely as a human observance, and therefore to no genuine effect. Conversely, as it is possible to try to handle the deity of Christ as a demonstrable truth of reason, and thus to eliminate the enlightenment of the Holy Spirit, so it is pos-

35. Luke 1:34, John 3:4,9.
36. Rom. 4:18.

sible to imagine an automatic divine working in the sacrament, and therefore to eliminate the Holy Spirit who alone disposes of this as of every means of grace. To be sure, there is nothing arbitrary or fortuitous about the relationship of the human action and the divine. But for the effect of baptism, this must neither be ignored on the one hand nor easily taken for granted on the other. Hence, baptism must always be administered and received with genuine prayer, and a readiness to see its meaning as revealed and applied by the Spirit.

Again, the effect of baptism is always linked with repentance and faith,[37] which is the baptismal response to the ultimate baptism of the death and resurrection of Christ. Baptism is a summons to acceptance of the death and resurrection of Jesus Christ in our place and stead. It cannot have its effect, therefore, without repentance and faith, which are this acceptance. In some cases, of course, it may work together with the word to evoke this response, for the effect cannot be rigorously tied in time to the administration, and the death and resurrection of Christ which is the primary significance of baptism are prior to any acceptance of ours. On the other hand, it may be a sign confirming repentance and faith and adding to their work. But in any case, this relationship is intrinsic to the whole outworking of the sacrament.

But the effect of the sacrament is not, of course, restricted to a single moment or period. It extends to the whole life of the Christian. This point has already emerged from a consideration of its meaning, for here again the effect is closely related to the meaning. Throughout our lives the one baptism has power to strengthen us with the reminder of Christ's substitutionary death and resurrection, to summon us to the further work of mortification and renewal, to reassure us in face of sickness and the inexorable march of death. To limit the effect of the sacrament to the period of conversion, or to think of it merely as a mysterious and not very obvious operation in infancy, is to miss the greater part of its efficacy.

In conclusion, we must again emphasize that there is always an irreducible element of mystery about baptism and its

37. Mark 16:16, Acts 2:38.

operation, as about all the works of the Holy Ghost. For, after all, how does the Holy Spirit work? How does He work through the word? Is it merely a psychological phenomenon? How does He work through His servants? Can it merely be explained in terms of human powers and activities? What is meant, not merely by repentance and faith which we perhaps think that we can understand, but by conviction of sin and regeneration? How do we come to see in Jesus of Nazareth the Son of the divine God? All these things take place in the human sphere, and are indeed a response to human activities. To that extent the operation of the word of God and baptism can be explained and stated in part, and in an important and indispensable part. We are not in the sphere of magic, or of sheer transcendence. Yet always there remains that even more important element, and the unity of the two aspects, which can be known, but cannot be explained or stated. The final secret of the operation of baptism, as of all the means of grace, is that of the Holy Spirit.

CHAPTER THREE

THE ADMINISTRATION OF BAPTISM

As ALREADY NOTED, the sacramental actions are basically very simple. In the case of baptism, what is involved is the application of water to the recipient in the triune name,[1] which is normally taken to mean with the accompanying words: "I baptize thee," or, "Be thou baptized, in the name of the Father, and of the Son, and of the Holy Ghost." No directions are given as to the details of the action either in the baptismal command or in accounts of baptisms in the New Testament.

The simplicity of the action and the lack of rubrics for its administration mean that there has been considerable freedom and therefore variety as to the performance of the essential rite. Naturally, it was not long before accepted modes of administration imposed themselves in the church, sometimes with biblical sanction, but always for the more impressive observance of so important a sign. Yet these forms had always to be subject both to the freedom of the action and the over-ruling authority of Scripture. In the present discussion, we shall attempt to see how the Reformers approached the questions of administration and why they made the decisions which in the main still control the service of baptism in the Reformation churches.

It was accepted, of course, that water must be the element used and the Reformers had no interest in the rather futile definitions of water or discussion of possible substitutes in case of its lack. It is true that on one occasion Luther caused no little stir by asserting that he would baptize in good

1. Matt. 28:19.

34

German beer if water were not present, but this was a characteristically Lutheran way of combating a sterile legalism. For the most part, the Reformers thought that water was as likely to be present as any liquid, and in its absence there was no such necessity of baptism as to require a substitute.

Any kind of water, whether in the sea, a river, a pool, a font or a bowl, was regarded as adequate for the purpose, as in the teaching of the Fathers. On the other hand, the Reformers preferred the administration in church, and since infants were normally the recipients they did not practice baptism in large bodies of water. Fonts were still used in some cases, but many of the more dogmatically Reformed favored baptism in a simple bowl or dish.

As will be seen, the amount of water used was not regarded as important. Nor was the mode of application. Most of the Reformers allowed that immersion was in some ways best calculated to bring out the meaning of the sign,[2] and this had of course been the common practice of the church for many centuries. Indeed, some of the churches, like the Church of England, made an attempt to retain "dipping" in the water. The tide of opinion, however, was against this method in almost all countries, and infusion and sprinkling were accepted as no less valid. It was commonly agreed that the recipient should go "under" the water, and therefore water was either poured or sprinkled on the head. Even the earlier Anabaptists did not attach significance to the mode, though the first immersion in the Rhine evoked admiration. The Reformers in particular did not see that full immersion was imposed either by the precept or precedent of Scripture, and therefore they found no dogmatic point at stake.

During the Middle Ages the practice had grown up of consecrating the water of baptism. This was normally done at Easter or Pentecost, the water being left in the font and renewed again only if occasion demanded. On the other hand, the presumed necessity of baptism had made it impossible to insist upon consecration, since emergency baptism had often to be administered with any water available. In lieu of consecration, the vessel used was then either given to the church or destroyed. Quite naturally, the Reformers took

2. Cf. Rom. 6:4.

the view that consecration was neither necessary nor scriptural, and since it gave rise to superstitious notions of baptismal efficacy among the ignorant they mostly attacked and discarded it, although in some churches, as in the Anglican, a dedicatory prayer was included to mark the setting aside of the water to its particular use. The addition of oil to the water as sometimes practiced was regarded as a clear addition to the element enjoined by Scripture and thus rejected.

Trine immersion was another point which called for some discussion. This was the practice of immersing, pouring or sprinkling three times instead of once. Various explanations have been advanced for the rise of this custom, including the association with the three persons of the Godhead and the recollection of the three days of Christ in the tomb. In effect, there is no particular reason why the one act of baptizing should not be threefold, but the Reformers took the sensible view that since it was not commanded in the Bible, it was better discontinued. The Church of England retained it in the first Prayer Book of 1549, but discarded it in 1552 and all subsequent revisions.

Together with trine immersion, many other customs were brought into the full service of baptism during the early and medieval periods. In the first instance, these usually had some spiritual meaning and helped to bring out a particular aspect of our salvation or of the new life in Christ. Thus, exorcism typified the expulsion of the devil, annointing the gift of the Holy Spirit, the baptismal robe our new righteousness in Christ, the mark of the cross enlistment to discipleship and warfare, the washing of the eyes the opening to spiritual understanding, and at an earlier time milk the new food of the Christian and the ten coins the ten commandments. It had always been realized of course, that these ceremonies were not essential to valid baptism, but a good deal of store was set by them, and even those privately baptized, if they survived, were expected to have a full service in ratification at a later date.

Basically, of course, there was nothing wrong in adding a meaningful ceremonial to the service, and many of the Reformers, including Jud and Zwingli as well as Luther and Cranmer, were at first tempted to retain some of the practices and to emphasize their evangelical significance. It was soon seen, however, that there were serious disadvantages in this course. For one thing, the ceremonies tended to obscure the real sign of baptism itself, rather than give it solemnity as at first intended. Again, superstitious notions could easily be associated with many of the practices, e.g., exorcism. And then, of course, there was always the consideration that the Bible itself did not mention any of these additional signs, and that it was better to keep to what was actually prescribed.

In point of fact, all the churches of the Reformed persuasion abolished the accompanying ceremonies altogether. The Church of England was an exception, for after the Lutheran pattern it retained just the one ceremony of marking with the sign of the cross — a practice which was defended against heated Puritan objections. In itself the point is not important. But it marked a difference of emphasis between the Anglican and other Reformed churches on points of church order and practice, the Anglican contending for a liberty of the church to institute or retain rites, etc., which are not contrary to Scripture, the Reformed insisting more narrowly that only that which is positively scriptural may be permitted. In this respect the Anglicans tended more in a Lutheran direction, although wholly at one with the Reformed in the doctrinal understanding.

In addition to the actual washing in water, baptismal administration had always included the recitation of the accompanying formula: "I baptize thee in the name of the Father, and of the Son, and of the Holy Ghost." In this respect, the Reformers were content to retain the common Western form instead of the Eastern "Be thou baptized." Their insistence upon the ancient decrees that the service should be in the language of the people saved them from the need to safeguard against ignorant or blasphemous priests such as those who were reported to have baptized in the name of the country *(patriae)* instead of the Father *(Patri)*, or to have added a reference to the devil to the threefold name of God.

The formula itself, however, was not regarded by the Reformers as a sufficient proclamation of the word of God, and therefore in administration in the Reformation churches provision is made for the reading of the Bible and for preaching, as well as for the common prayer of the congregation. This is done in various ways. The Church of England, for example, following the Lutheran method, has a fairly full service of baptism which includes prayer, a Gospel passage, and a good deal of exhortation. In addition, the Anglicans agree with the rest of the Reformed that baptism should normally take place at a time of public worship and within the setting of an ordinary service; and it is recommended that opportunity should be taken to declare the meaning of the sacrament and to drive home its message. All the Reformation churches agree, as we have seen, that the service must be in the language of the people, since the use of a language which at best is only dimly understood by the majority can only be an unnecessary barrier to the effective operation of the sacrament. It is worth noting, by the way, that in the Lutheran and Anglican service a tremendous stress is laid upon the prayer of the congregation on behalf of those who are to receive the sacrament, and this too is essential to its proper and therefore effective administration.

The emphasis upon the need for a genuine administration of the word of God, and therefore for setting baptism in the context of public worship, led the Reformed churches to insist that baptism must never be administered privately in the home, or even in a semi-private service in church. In principle, this was wholly right. Baptism is not a private affair, but something which concerns the whole congregation to which the person baptized is admitted. And it is essential that there should normally be a true proclamation of the word of God at the time of its administration. Even the plea of necessity is not decisive, for there is no absolute necessity of the rite to eternal salvation.

At the same time, the banning of private services in certain cases was never accepted by the Church of England, and it has continued or has been restored in other churches of the Reformed persuasion. The reasons in its favor may be briefly stated. First, the Bible itself does not limit baptismal administration to times of public worship. Second, a private baptism can be ratified in a public service. Third, even though there is no absolute necessity, there is a necessity to do what is commanded, i.e., to baptize. And finally, baptism itself is more important than the order of its administration. To be sure, it ought normally to take place in public. But where this is impossible and there is imminent danger of death, it is better that the sign should be given than withheld for a scruple of order. These considerations do not usually apply in the case of adults, and the Anglicans agree with the other Reformed that adult baptisms should take place with the greatest solemnity, the bishop himself being the minister if at all possible.

The question of private baptisms is linked with that of lay-baptisms, or baptisms by women, and therefore a word might be said at this point on the general question of the minister. In the first flush of the Reformation the emphasis on the priesthood of the laity carried with it a possible depreciation of the orderly ministry, and Luther and those who followed him were insistent upon the rights of ordinary believers to minister the word and sacraments where circumstances demanded. On the Reformed side, however, there was a clear recognition of the need for order in these matters, and in the normal life of the church no place could be found for what some of the earlier Puritans called "meddling in ministers' matters." This emerged particularly in relation to baptism, where the laity had traditionally acted in cases of emergency. But this was strictly forbidden in the Reformed churches, and the insistence upon public administration helped to enforce the prohibition.

The matter was not quite so clear in England, however, and the whole question of the minister called for considerable discussion. On the one side, there were those who attacked even the administering of baptism by deacons, on the ground that these were not genuine ministers of the word and sacraments. But the example of Philip seemed to meet this objection.[3] More seriously, the retention of private baptism meant that women continued to baptize in England for some years after the Reformation Settlement. But after prolonged discussion, it was eventually decided that while private baptism should be retained, it should be given only by a minister; and from 1604 onward this has been the only lawful practice in the Church of England — so much so, indeed, that some Anglicans later rejected as invalid the administrations of dissenting ministers. In favor of baptism by women it was argued

3. Acts 8:38.

that the sacrament is more important than the minister, that charity must take precedence over law, that anyone may give what he has received, and that the wife of Moses administered circumcision in the Old Testament.[4] Against this it was pointed out that there are few cases when a minister cannot be had, that Zipporah's isolated and perhaps rather injudicious action cannot be made the basis of a regular practice, and that while the sacrament should be given if at all possible there is no absolute necessity of baptism to salvation.

The insistence upon public baptism, or upon private baptism as required only by a minister, does not mean an encouragement of laxity in relation to the sacrament. On the contrary, the Reformation churches see a high necessity to do what the Lord commanded, and therefore they bring before their adherents the need either to receive baptism themselves, or to bring their children to baptism, at the earliest possible moment. No laws are laid down, as in the medieval church; but neglect of a means of grace ordained by God Himself gives obvious evidence of an unbelieving and disobedient spirit.

In the case of adults, the common practice is to administer baptism only after a fairly prolonged period of instruction in which care is taken to see that the recipient understands the Gospel and can make a conscientious profession of repentance, faith, and obedience. This follows the custom of the early church with its long catechumenate culminating in the great baptisms of Easter and Pentecost. To be sure, there are examples of more rapid baptism in the New Testament, but these are associated with very obvious outpourings of the Holy Spirit.[5] Adults are naturally expected to express their desire for baptism and to make a personal confession of faith. Exceptions may be allowed in the case of the mentally ill, but the Reformers do not lay down any precise procedure for such cases (as attempted in the Middle Ages), since it is not felt that they are in any case excluded from the divine mercy by inability to have a conscious faith.

Where infants are baptized, professing parents are urged to bring them to baptism as soon as may conveniently be arranged. It is essential that there should be Christians to

4. Exod. 4:24.
5. Acts 2:41, 8:38, 9:18, 10:48.

sponsor them — either the parents themselves, or relatives or friends — since their title to the sacrament rests on their descent from professing Christians, and provision must be made for their instruction in the response which baptism demands. In most of the Reformed churches the parents themselves present their own children, and undertake the duty of bringing them up in Christian faith and obedience. In the Church of England, however, the medieval practice of sponsors or god-parents is retained, and instead of professing their own faith these make a profession in the name of the infant until he is old enough to answer for himself (which is done, of course, in confirmation). This professing for the infant has been variously understood. Some take it as a vicarious profession either by the sponsors or by the church of which they are the representatives. Some go to the opposite extreme and see in it not much more than a personal profession. The midway position is probably the true one, that the sponsors stand surety for the future repentance, faith, and obedience of the child, undertaking by prayer and instruction to bring it to a personal fulfillment as it grows to years of understanding.

Already at an early period a question arose which has recently caused a good deal of stir in some countries, that of indiscriminate baptism. Ought the sacrament to be administered where one of the parents, and perhaps both, are living in obvious indifference and even flagrant sinfulness? On the face of it, does it not seem to be an empty mockery of the divine ordinance where this is the case? Yet a little thought shows that the sin or indifference of the parent or parents is not a valid reason for withholding baptism so long as they are prepared to make a profession of Christian faith and to ensure the Christian upbringing of the child. For one thing, the child is not responsible. For another, we are not to anticipate the last judgment and pronounce on the sincerity of the profession made. Third, the sacrament is supremely a sacrament of the saving work of Christ, which extends to all men, and is indeed supremely for sinners. And finally, if there is a Christian descent, God has promised His mercies, not for one or two, but for a thousand generations.[6] Certainly, the church has every right to bring unsatisfactory parents

6. Deut. 7:9.

under its discipline. Certainly, it has every right to insist that there be a serious attempt at Christian instruction. But it is another matter to exercise discrimination in the granting of baptism itself where it is desired for the children of parents who have made a Christian profession, and the Reformers rightly argue that where there is the desire, and the Christian faith has not completely perished, the means of grace ought not to be used as an instrument of discipline.

With their insistence upon an orderly public administration, the Reformed churches are saved from quite a number of detailed and rather legalistic problems which called for discussion in the Middle Ages. For example, there is no need to enter into the complicated and delicate problem of prenatal baptism. Again, the question of doubtful baptisms does not arise, and therefore there is no need for conditional baptism. Even in England, where baptism is to be by a minister and registers are to be kept, the possibility of cases of doubt is reduced to a minimum.

It is also worth noting in this connection that the problems which gave rise to a doctrine of intention are dispelled. Obviously, if baptism may be administered by laymen, and even in a pinch by well-disposed heathens, the question arises whether they really intend to give Christian baptism, or even whether a copy of the ceremony by children at play does not constitute a true baptism. And the way is thus opened up for a full-scale discussion of intention, with all the difficulties and uncertainties to which it gives rise. But when a properly ordained minister baptizes before the congregation, whatever may be the secret intentions or dispositions of his heart, it may be reasonably presupposed that he is doing what he is ordained to do, and no problem of intention arises. In any case, the validity and power of the sacrament do not rest in the human minister, but in the true Minister, God Himself, the Father, Son and Holy Spirit. It is for this reason that in spite of the erroneous beliefs of Romanism, the baptism which it administers can be accepted as true baptism, and the retention of the sacrament regarded as a mark of the persistence of the true church through all the errors and superstitions.

A brief word may be said in conclusion about two other abuses of baptism which are avoided in Reformation practice.

The first concerns the enforced baptism of unbelievers or their children, whether by duress, kidnapping or stratagem. This is plainly contrary to the whole meaning and work of the sacrament, for while the sacrifice of Jesus Christ is for all, there is no question of its being forced upon all, and acceptance in repentance and faith is the obvious objective of the ministry of word and sacrament. To be fair, it must be stated that the reputable medieval theologians were opposed to enforced baptisms, and efforts were made to prevent them. But in many cases the doctrine of an absolute necessity of the sacrament and the desire for spiritual aggrandizement were too strong for the official teaching and policy. In the Reformation churches, however, the temptation has hardly arisen, for while those who have not heard the Gospel are not necessarily excluded from salvation, it is plainly seen that the sacrament is only for those within the external covenant, and an orderly administration prevents irregularities of this kind.

The second abuse concerns the application of baptism to such inanimate objects as flags and bells — a common and lucrative practice in the Middle Ages. Again, it must be allowed that this was not regarded as baptism in the strict sense. Yet if it is not true baptism, it is a parody and therefore quite out of place. And to surround it with more pomp and circumstance than true baptism is to foster a wrong sense of proportion. For these reasons, and because of the financial abuses and superstitions involved, and a high sense of the dignity of the sacrament, the Reformed churches have always been strongly opposed to any such misapplication.

CHAPTER FOUR

PROBLEMS OF BAPTISM

———

IN THE COURSE OF CENTURIES it is only natural that many
strange ideas and erroneous opinions should have grown up
in relation to baptism. Some of these may be discounted at
once. For example, the attempt to replace baptism in water
by a literal baptism with fire (by branding)[1] is plainly
ridiculous, as is also the demand that on the model of Jesus
no one should be baptized except at the age of thirty.[2] The
notion that baptismal water acquires an almost magical
power as the vehicle of grace is also an exaggeration which
is not supported in serious theology, although there are
tendencies in this direction in the Middle Ages, especially in
association with consecration. Indeed, it may well be that
only the supposed absolute necessity of baptism prevented
the rise of a definite equivalent to the eucharistic doctrine
of transubstantiation.

On the other hand, two of the errors are more powerful
and persistent, and at the same time rather less obvious, so
that even today we must try to understand them if we are to
find our way to an appreciation of the Reformation teaching
and above all to a doctrine and practice which are truly
biblical. These aberrations are very different in nature, but
they are distinguished by the common feature that they
"subjectivize" the sacrament, transferring the center or focus
of interest and operation from the work done by Christ on
behalf of the baptized to the work done in the baptized
themselves. At root, therefore, they owe their origin to a

1. On the basis of Matt. 3:11.
2. Cf. Luke 3:23.

failure to appreciate the substitutionary nature of the death and resurrection of Jesus Christ, and even though they intend to be biblical in their own way, and in varying degrees achieve this, they miss the very heart of the Gospel and therefore misunderstand the sacrament of the Gospel. It is in virtue of their penetration to the core of the saving work of God in substitution and justification that the Reformers are able to point us to a true doctrine of baptism and to the consequent practice.

The first form of this subjectivization is to be found in the doctrine which grew up in the Middle Ages, and which carried with it a number of associated errors. In its own way, this teaching was meant to be extremely objective. It insisted that all the blessings of baptism rest upon the work accomplished by Christ. And it claimed that, whatever may be the instruments of His operation, these blessings are granted only by the Holy Spirit. But through a failure to see the true and radical nature of substitution, and the resultant misunderstanding of justification, it was thought that the real work of baptism is done in the baptized. It is they who are inwardly cleansed from sin. It is they whose old life is brought to an end. It is they who, in virtue of Christ's work and the operation of the Spirit through baptism, are made just. It is they who begin a new life. And because the work of Christ is done, and it is the sovereign Spirit who is at work, we can count on it that this real work of baptism will take place in them, so that the baptized person, at the moment of baptism, is no longer a sinner deserving in himself the wrath and punishment of God, but a spotless saint, washed from every stain of sin and endowed with graces to enable him to persevere in the new life which he himself has now actually begun.

Of course, it is not quite so mechanical as it sounds, or as it is sometimes represented in Protestant polemics. In the case of adults, there is required sincerity of heart and therefore some measure of repentance and faith before the sacrament can have its effect of inward cleansing and renewal. But the fact remains that baptism is thought of supremely in subjective terms as a work within the recipient, and that its operation is interpreted causally as the producing of a given effect by a given cause so long as there is no obstacle such as insincerity to hinder it. When we come to infant baptism, and no obstacle can be opposed, the working becomes wholly automatic, and in this view it may be taken for granted that the great work of the Holy Spirit has taken place in each of the recipients of baptism, so that if they die without committing further sin they will not only be safe from hell, but will go straight to heaven with no intervening period of purgatorial cleansing.

Now the Reformers do not dispute the main presuppositions of this error, that baptism must be related to the work of Christ, that its operation is by the Holy Spirit, and that we can count upon what God does on our behalf. Nor do they reject the view that baptism is a means of grace, and that God makes use of it as such. But with their renewed understanding of justification, and therefore their return to a serious doctrine of substitution, they cut right across the subjectivizing which perverts the medieval view. The true work of baptism is the work which is done for us, not in us. It is not we who literally die and rise again, but Jesus Christ, the One for the many,[3] and we by faith in Him. It is not we who are righteous, but we are counted righteous in Jesus Christ,[4] being righteous only because the life which we now live by the faith of Christ,[5] and faith in Him, is our reality before God and therefore in truth. Once this is grasped, then the whole emphasis on a subjective work is seen to be false, and the notion of a causal operation drops away of itself, being replaced by that of grace, and the word of grace, and the grateful response of penitence and faith.

A first consequence of this sacramentalist subjectivization of baptism is that the eternal rite becomes absolutely necessary to salvation. Since a work has to be done in the individual, it is obvious that there can be no salvation without this cleansing and renewal. But since the means appointed for the accomplishment of this work is baptism, there can be no salvation, or at least no assurance of salvation, without the proper means of grace.[6] The rule is not quite so rigid as might appear. From very early times it had been accepted

3. II Cor. 5:14.
4. Rom. 3:24.
5. Gal. 2:20.
6. John 3:5 was taken in this sense.

that martyrdom supplies the lack of baptism, or even a genuine conversion of heart where there is no possibility of receiving the sacrament. These may be regarded as a baptism of blood and a baptism of the Spirit respectively, and water goes hand in hand with blood and the Spirit to give the threefold witness.[7] But in the case of infants in a settled Christian community these two alternatives are normally ruled out. Hence, it is of supreme importance that infants should be baptized. If they are not, there can be no hope of heaven in any true sense, and while many Roman Catholic theologians will allow unbaptized infants a modified hell or a kind of mediate state or lesser heaven, the stricter consign them to eternal torment. In these circumstances we can understand the need for private baptism or baptism by women in cases of emergency, and the atmosphere of superstitious awe and terror with which the sacrament of grace is so often regarded by the ignorant.

As we may readily suppose, the Reformers will have nothing of this absolute necessity of the sacrament, not because they are swayed by sentimentality, but because they see that it is based on a misunderstanding. They are jealous for the honor of baptism, and thus contend for the true necessity, which is a necessity of precept. Christ Himself has ordained the sacrament for our benefit, and therefore we must not despise or neglect it. They also see the absolute necessity of the baptismal work. Without this work there can indeed be no hope of salvation. But the real work of baptism is not a subjective work in us; it is the objective work accomplished in Christ for us. And although baptism as a means of grace can further our acceptance of this work and response to it in repentance and faith, lack of the sacrament for any reason but willful contempt and neglect cannot be regarded as a reason for eternal perdition. In the case of infants, where there can be no conscious acceptance and response in any case, the Reformers are fully persuaded that the work attested and sealed in baptism, the reconciling work of the Son in fulfillment of the covenant of the Father, avails irrespective of the external administration, though the rite obviously has its own dignity and value as a witness to this truth, and as a summons to the baptized to the appropriate acceptance

7. I John 5:8.

and response as he grows to years of understanding. The change is clearly reflected in the statement at the end of the Anglican Order of Public Baptism. This gives the assurance that baptized children are undoubtedly saved (in virtue of the gracious promise of Christ to which appeal is made earlier in the service). But it omits the crucial words "and else not" which in earlier formularies had made it plain that the unbaptized cannot hope for salvation (notwithstanding the divine work and promise).

A second consequence is just as serious, for although baptism is seen to be so necessary, and although it accomplishes so wonderful a work, its results are inevitably limited. The work in us is quickly undone once the baptized goes out into the world and is faced by temptation and commits actual sin. To be sure, a good deal of benefit remains. So long as the sin is not "mortal," security from hell is guaranteed. And the infused graces are at hand to give some help in face of temptation. But for all that, concupiscence remains as a continual liability to sin, and in actual fact the cleansed soul is very quickly blotted and stained, and the prospect opens up of a lengthy and painful period of cleansing. In other words, the baptized is given a fresh start, and some help on the way. But the Christian life then becomes a struggle to maintain the ground won, and a search for means to avoid the consequences when this struggle is unsuccessful. In these circumstances, it is only natural that for all its urgent necessity, baptism should come to mean very little in practice, especially for those baptized in infancy. It is the essential beginning, but it is only an almost legendary beginning when for a brief moment sanctity is enjoyed. It has no very obvious significance, however, in the far more urgent and pressing problems of the Christian faced with the prospect of purgatory or even perdition.

By linking baptism supremely with the once-for-all and all-sufficient work of Christ, the Reformers restored to it its true dignity and importance. If it is the sacrament of something done in us, then obviously its significance is local. But as the sacrament of the substitutionary work of Christ, its significance is for the whole life of the Christian. The obedience and sacrifice and resurrection of Christ avail for good and all. If we are justified in Christ, not in ourselves, we cannot cease to be justified. If we can say that Christ is our wisdom and sanctification,[8] there need be no fear that the promised gifts of grace can be lost. We can refuse to accept them. We can turn away from them. We can make a poor response to them. But the gifts which Christ has won for us, and which are attested in Christ, are finally secured. Hence, there need be no doubt or vacillation in the Christian life; but even in the moments of deepest failure we can turn to baptism, to the baptismal work behind the sign, and see there our comfort and strength.

But finally, since baptism is quickly robbed of its full effect by fresh sin, there arises the problem of post-baptismal sin, or rather, of the means of its forgiveness or alleviation. And it is very largely in answer to this problem that the whole medieval system arises with all its monstrous abuses. The most blatant need is where there is deadly sin, e.g., an offence against the Ten Commandments, and therefore the soul is again brought under the judgment of hell. But even where lesser sins are committed, definite penalties are supposed to be incurred which, because they are temporal, are not covered by the sacrifice of Christ, so that unless they can be mitigated they will have to be carried by the sinner through longer or shorter periods of purgatory. Either way, it will be seen that for all the great benefits of baptism the Christian is caught in a situation in which he must find new means of relief. Nor is the urgency much less acute where only temporal punishment is at stake, for the prospect of purgatory is hardly more attractive than that of hell itself.

The answer to this problem of post-baptismal sin gives us many of the worst elements in medieval practice. Penance forms a second plank of salvation where mortal sin is committed, inferior to baptism in the fullness of its effects, but more useful in the fact that it can be repeated. Originally designed specifically for more serious cases, penance can also supply some relief from the fancied pains of purgatory (which is itself a product of this whole misunderstanding). Out of the need for penance there arises the whole system of auricular confession with its attendant evils. In addition, relief is to be sought from the receiving of communion, the saying and paying of masses, the intercession of the saints,

8. I Cor. 1:30.

transfers from the treasury of merit, i.e., the superabundant merits of Christ and the saints, the practice of almsgiving, pilgrimages, and the like. A further trouble about this whole system is that no one ever knows how he really stands in respect to purgatory, and the result is a situation of uncertainty and terror which is easily exploited for purposes of oppression or enrichment.

The greatness of the Reformers is that with the biblical understanding of justification, and therefore their realization that the true work of baptism is the work of Christ for us rather than a subjective cleansing, they destroy these errors and abuses at the very root. Naturally, there is no minimizing of post-baptismal sin. On the contrary, the Reformers view it with even greater seriousness than the medieval scholars and the theologians of Trent. They see that the baptized man is always in himself a sinner. It is only in Christ that he is righteous. Even the root of sin remains within him. He does not merely have a tendency to sin which is not in itself sinful. Concupiscence itself has the nature of sin, even in the regenerate. And it will naturally issue in acts of sin, sometimes more serious and sometimes less, so that the outworking of sanctification is a life-long task for the Christian. But the fact remains that no problem of atonement or remission is posed by these fresh acts of sin. No new means are required to relieve from their eternal or supposed temporal penalties. For if it is only in Christ that the believer is righteous, this means that he is genuinely and perfectly and finally righteous. As Luther so finely put it, he is at one and the same time both sinful and righteous. And his new and true reality is his being in Christ, and therefore his righteousness. This is what is attested and sealed in baptism.

In these circumstances, there is no problem of post-baptismal sin in the traditional sense. The work objectively accomplished in Jesus Christ cannot be offset or weakened by the action of the recipient. And there is no subjective status effected by the sacrament to be lost or impaired. The only problem of the post-baptismal sinner is that it is a denial of the true reality of the believer, a refusal to be what he is in Christ, or to act as such. But baptism itself is the continuing answer to this problem. It shows him what has been done vicariously in Christ as the One for the many.

It points him to the forgiveness and renewal which are there in Christ. It summons him to constant repentance and faith, mortification and renewal, and in this way to responsive acceptance of what he is, in virtue of the substitutionary work of Christ. Whether or not he can finally fall from Christ is another matter. On the whole, with their tremendous emphasis on the election of the Father, the substitution of the Son, and the sovereign work of the Spirit, the Reformers do not think so. But even if the sinner does, it can only be a falling away from this true reality, a refusal finally to enter into it and correspond to it. And in his ultimate salvation the elect will not be able to point to a work, or a series of works, accomplished in himself, but to the once-for-all work accomplished outside himself and on his behalf by God Himself, as attested and sealed in the sacrament.

This, then, is the first form of the subjectivization of the sacrament, and the answer of Reformation doctrine to it. But the trouble is that unless there is a solid grounding in the Bible this first form with its abuses has a tendency to evoke the reaction of a second subjectivization, which is free from many of the attendant evils, which is more true to Scripture in its portrayal of the subjective process, but which is no less false in its emphasis and therefore misleading in its understanding of baptism. This reaction seems to have begun already in some of the pre-Reformation sects, but it is most clearly seen in the Anabaptist doctrine of the 16th century. And since the Anabaptist movement has found permanent form in the Protestant world, and has been given an added fillip in Evangelical circles by the subjectivist forces of Pietism and Romantic Liberalism, it will be worth our while to consider the basic criticism brought against it by the Reformers.

Like the sacramentalist error, the Anabaptist one does not intend to depreciate the work of Christ. On the contrary, it realizes that there can be no salvation without this work. It also allows that the application of this work is ultimately to be attributed to the operation of the Holy Spirit. At the same time, it avoids the blatant evils associated with the earlier form. It does not regard baptism as a quasi-mechanical means of grace. It has no thought of making it absolutely necessary to salvation. It is careful to link baptism and salvation with the repentance and faith which are clearly demanded in the Bible, and which have always been brought into conjunction with the sacrament. Indeed, so rigorous is it in opposition to the earlier errors that it will not allow baptism without a profession of repentance and faith, so that there can be no question of an empty sacramentalism. The insistence upon repentance and faith also ensures that the baptismal work cannot be thought of in terms of a sanctification accomplished in us, but is related to the justification which we have in Jesus Christ. Hence, it might appear — and this is how the Anabaptists themselves understood it — that Anabaptist teaching and practice is a logical development of the Reformation, and that it discards features which the leading Reformers unfortunately retained.

But the Reformers saw that behind all the detailed exegetical differences there are serious theological objections to Anabaptism. Its basic error is to find the true work of baptism, not in the reconciling work of Christ, but in our own movement of repentance and faith. In this way it subjectivizes the sacrament no less than the medieval doctrine. To be sure, there is no actual making righteous. But there is a movement of repentance and faith which is the real dying and rising again of baptism. It is to this that the sacrament bears witness. It is this which it summons us to work out. It is this which occupies the center of the stage when the sacrament is administered. It is this which cannot be seen or attested in infants, so that they are naturally disqualified as recipients. That we are dead and risen again in Christ is only a background truth, as in the Middle Ages. What counts is that we ourselves die and rise again, that we repent and believe, or at least profess to do so. And this, of course, is all out of proportion. That there is demanded a response of repentance and faith which corresponds to the death and resurrection of Christ could nowhere be more finely emphasized than in the works of the Reformers. But they insist that baptism is not primarily a sacrament of repentance and faith, or anything that we do, or anything that takes place in us, but of the vicarious death and resurrection of Christ for our forgiveness and renewal, of what God does, and of what He does in His Son.

The serious consequences (or causes) of the Anabaptist subjectivization are clearly seen in many of their associated beliefs. Since these cover so wide a sphere, and are related to baptism only indirectly, they may be briefly summarized in the present context. To begin with, the Anabaptists depreciated the Old Testament, largely because they failed to see in it the movement of the electing God instituting His covenant and preparing its fulfillment. For this reason, they naturally could not see the close relationship between baptism and election (and also circumcision), especially in connection with infants. Again, they could find no place for original sin, for with the stress upon individual death and resurrection rather than upon the substitutionary dying and rising again of the One for the many, it is natural that they should not understand the solidarity of the race in sin.

Not unnaturally they were Pelagian also in their understanding of the response to the Gospel, for since the prior work of Father, Son, and Holy Spirit in election, substitution, and sovereign application was pushed into the background, it was inevitable that the decision of the individual, and therefore his freedom to decide, should be emphasized. No doubt all that man had to do was simply to believe, to accept what he could not do for himself, what God had done. But the fact remained that this last step of acceptance, of decision, of personal faith, was the real step to salvation. And this was something which only he could do, so that in the whole presentation of the Gospel, as in the administration of the sacrament, there was a Pelagian stress.

Of a piece with this was their rationalizing of faith. As they saw it, faith is possible only where there is self-awareness. It is impossible in the case of infants. But this kind of impossibility is only the rational impossibility which provokes Mary and Nicodemus to ask how these things can be. It can be argued only when it is forgotten that faith is the work of the Holy Spirit, who can fill the infant John no less than the adult Cornelius.[9] It stands in flat contradiction to the call of the Gospel, which is not that we should become adults but children.[10] It is not the real impossibility, namely, that sinners should understand the things of God without the

9. Luke 1:15.
10. Matt. 19:3.

enlightenment of the Holy Ghost.[11] And it robs those who
die in infancy of any hope of salvation, unless the full logic
of Pelagianism is accepted and they are regarded as innocent
in themselves and able to be pleasing to God without faith.

Finally, linking baptism with the work of the believer
rather than that of God, the Anabaptists rob it of its true
significance as a sacrament of the Gospel. At the very most
it can only be an external sign witnessing to the faith of the
individual, giving him a certain emotional satisfaction, and
pledging him to Christian conduct. It loses its true honor
and power as a sacrament of the substitutionary work of
Christ. And in certain circumstances, for all that it may be
magnified by its reservation for professing believers and perhaps a striking mode of administration, it may well come to
be thought of as dispensable. For, after all, the thing attested
or signified, the repentance and faith of the individual,
cannot be brought into any strict relationship with the
ordinance. It is not for nothing that some of the extremer
Anabaptists dismissed baptism altogether as childish play
unnecessary for mature Christians. The dismissal or depreciation is the more serious because it is so evidently linked with
a desire to "spiritualize" Christianity, to make it a religion
of pure inwardness, to loosen its contacts with material
reality, in a word, to contest the incarnational duality of the
means and work of grace, and ultimately therefore to deny
that the Word really took human flesh of the Virgin.

Many who follow the Anabaptists in their insistence that
baptism should not be given except on profession of faith
will not, of course, subscribe to their associated tenets. It may
be argued, therefore, that the defense of the Reformers
against them has only historical interest. But two points are
worth remembering before we rush hastily to this conclusion.

The first is that, although the form has changed, these
beliefs are substantially those which have dominated Protestant Liberalism during the last two centuries and more. It is
characteristic of this whole movement that the Old Testament should in various ways be set on a lower plane than
the New and in some sense isolated from it; that the very
idea of original sin should be dismissed with horror; that

11. I Cor. 2:14.

acceptance of the grace of God should be made a matter of the free choice of the individual will; that notions such as election, substitution, and sovereignty should be revised, reinterpreted, or rejected; that the whole understanding of Christianity itself, and therefore of faith, should be rationalized; that there should be a movement in the direction of a religion of pure spirit; and that sacramental observances should be retained at best only as symbolical acts with a certain psychological usefulness. And while Evangelical Protestants will naturally resist these doctrines in their blatant form, they have always to ask themselves whether consciously or unconsciously, openly or secretly, they have not come under their sway and allowed them a certain entry.

The second is that subjectivism is the cause or consequence of all these errors, that it has undoubtedly made an effective penetration into the Evangelical world, and that it still finds expression and support in the subjectivization of baptism by Baptists and by those who administer infant baptism only with a rather muddled head or uneasy conscience. While we must be careful not to exaggerate, a study of much modern evangelism, piety, and hymnology reveals how serious the influence upon Evangelicalism has been of the combined forces of Pietism, Schleiermacher, and Kant, e.g., in the emphasis upon the centrality of decision, upon the believer and his emotional state, and even upon psychological procedures. Biblical material is used, but with an emphasis and proportion very different from those of the Bible, so that the result is very far from biblical. For a theology cannot be genuinely biblical, however sound its doctrine of Scripture or however strict its use of scriptural material, if it achieves an emphasis which is subjective and therefore anthropological rather than objective and therefore christological and theological. To be sure, this emphasis is to be found in much wider than Baptist circles. But it emerges with peculiar distinctness when baptism is made a sign of our work rather than that of the Trinity on our behalf, and even nominally it becomes "believers'" baptism rather than the baptism of the Lord.

Against the associated errors of Anabaptism and contemporary Liberalism, as against the subjectivism which is their root or result, the Reformers stand firmly for a gen-

uinely biblical view, and they thus see the meaning and
legitimacy of the baptism of the infants of professing Christians. In the first instance, they cannot divide the Testaments,
for the electing and covenant-making God of the Old is the
God who has fulfilled the covenant in the New. Thus baptism is no less a covenant sign than circumcision. The blood
has been removed, the sign is retrospective, the scope has
been widened, but as the sacrament of election, it cannot be
withheld from children.[12]

Again, they must take seriously the fact that there is a sin
of the race as well as of individuals, and therefore they can
take seriously a reconciliation of the race accomplished in
the one sin-bearing Representative and His death and resurrection in our place and on our behalf.[13] Hence baptism
may be administered no less to infants than to adult con-
fessors as a sacrament not only of their election but also of
their reconciliation in Christ,[14] so long as they belong to a
circle in which they will be instructed in its meaning. Again,
they see that any movement of ours in repentance and faith
can only be a response to the prior movement of God, and
that even this response can be made only in the power of the
Holy Spirit.[15] Far more basic than the response, therefore, is
the work which evokes it, and since it is this prior work
which baptism proclaims and of which it is a means, its
administration need not be restricted to those in whom we
think to see the response, or whom we judge capable of it.

Again, they do not regard this response as in any sense a
human possibility, and therefore rational in character. It
takes a human form, since it is the response of men. But its
true nature evades psychological study. Even, and perhaps
especially, in adults, it is the mystery of the life-giving Spirit.
And since it is not for us to say when or where or in what
circumstances the Spirit should commence and further His
work, we have no warrant for refusing to infants within the
church the sacrament which is its seal and instrument.

To those who read the Bible through the spectacles of
modern subjectivism, the Reformers' defense of infant bap-

12. Cf. Acts 2:39, I Cor. 7:14.
13. Rom. 5:12ff.
14. II Cor. 5:14ff.
15. I Cor. 2:10ff.

tism may seem muddled, strange, and almost inexplicable. But the point is that they do not make the mistake of opposing to the sacramentalist subjectivism of the Middle Ages an Evangelical version of the same error. Instead, they call both errors back to the underlying and objective truth which both assume, but which in varying degrees they allow to be crowded out. In other words, they call them back from their interest in what is done in us, whether automatically or by our own decision, to the more basic interest in what is done for us, the election of the Father fulfilled in the substitution of the Son and brought to us by the sovereign work of the Spirit. In this way, the true meaning and power of baptism are revealed, the legitimacy and challenge of infant baptism are perceived, and the whole theology, preaching, and life of the church are given their proper basis and center.

CHAPTER FIVE

THE LORD'S SUPPER

LIKE BAPTISM, the second of the two dominical or evangelical sacraments consists in what is basically a very simple action, the taking of bread and wine by assembled Christians in remembrance of the death and resurrection of the Lord. Many possible models have been found for this rite, for common meals have often been invested with religious significance, especially in the context of sacrifice. On the other hand, there can be no doubt that this particular action originates with the direct institution of the Lord Himself,[1] and that it is modeled upon the passover within which it is set[2] and in replacement of which it forms the second of the two signs of the new covenant. Not a great deal is said explicitly about it in Acts and Epistles, but the possible references at the beginning of Acts (namely, in the breaking of bread)[3] and the discussion in I Corinthians[4] make it plain that the first disciples did actually "do this" as the Lord commanded, and there are various other allusions in the course of the New Testament.

As in the case of baptism, but much more patently, the Lord's Supper brings us into direct relationship with the very core and center of Christianity in the reconciling work of Jesus Christ, and particularly in His self-offering for us in suffering and death. This is foreshadowed in the reference of Jesus to the cup which He is going to drink, the cup being the Old Testament figure for suffering and judgment. Thus

1. Matt. 26:26ff.
2. Matt. 26:17ff.
3. Acts 2:46.
4. I Cor. 11:23ff.

He asks the sons of Zebedee whether they can drink the cup which He shall drink.[5] It is also confirmed by the prayer of Gethsemane, when He asks that if it be possible He may be spared this bitter cup.[6] In the institution itself the connection is very forcibly made when He speaks of the bread as His body to be broken for His people,[7] and the wine or cup as His blood to be outpoured.[8] In other words, the cross and passion are the real action underlying the external sign, and the Lord's Supper is a witness and reflection of this basic work, an enacted, visible, and tangible sign to bring home its truth and reality to the participants.

But this means that when the believer comes to this Supper he is pointed once again to the saving action of the Trinity as this found its center in the death of Jesus Christ. It is again the work of the whole Trinity which is attested. If Jesus Christ takes and drinks the cup, it is in final obedience to the electing will of the Father, causing the rejection which we had merited to fall on the beloved Son, but in this way enabling His people to be elected with Him. The Son Himself is the One in whom this loving plan and purpose of God is fulfilled, and it is in the power of the eternal Spirit that He offers Himself to the Father,[9] and by the Spirit that this work is presented to us for acceptance and response. The showing forth[10] of this work in the sacrament is again a summons to repentance and faith, so that instances are not lacking of those who have been brought to conversion within the setting of its administration. But primarily it is for the confirmation and strengthening of faith. The center of the divine work in the passion of Christ is vividly called to mind, and its meaning declared. By this proclamation of the cross the believer is reassured of the forgiveness of his sins, and enthused afresh by the thought of the amazing love which could plan and accomplish so much at so great a cost.

It is worth noting in this respect that, although it is not primary, the subjective element is rather stronger in the case

5. Matt. 20:22.
6. Matt. 26:42.
7. Luke 22:19.
8. Matt. 26:28.
9. Heb. 9:14.
10. I Cor. 11:26.

of the Supper than in that of baptism. In baptism the recipient does not baptize himself, although one or two of the earlier Baptists unconsciously carried their subjectivization to its logical extreme by doing this. In normal circumstances, he is baptized. But in the Supper he is invited to take and eat. This is particularly appropriate in the second and continuing sacrament, for when the love of God has laid hold of us we are invited to respond by making it our own, and thus to draw on the strength and benefits which are proffered by it. The Lord Jesus gave His body and blood for us. In so doing, He accomplished our forgiveness and renewal. These are signed and sealed to us in baptism. And now we are constantly to make these gifts our own, to accept the body and blood of Christ offered for us, to receive the crucified and risen Christ as our true life, to draw our sustenance from Him, to be built up in faith and fortified for obedience and service by the remembrance of His work. No one else can take for us; each must eat and drink for himself.

The thought of the strengthening and nourishment of faith, indeed of the whole Christian life of the believer, is naturally contained in the action. As the breaking of the bread and the pouring of the wine are well adapted to signify the self-offering of Christ, so the taking of the bread and drinking of the cup clearly bring before us the fact that we must feed on Christ and His work.[11] Thus, even though it is we who must take and eat, the real emphasis is on the fact that we are weak and perishing in ourselves, and wholly dependent upon this sustenance. In other words, it is the food which is of primary importance. Nor must the thought of nourishment be isolated from that of sacrifice. We do not just feed on Christ in a vaguely metaphorical way, or on Christ in general. We feed on the crucified and risen Christ,[12] and therefore here, too, the basic thought is not assimilation but substitution. This body and blood were offered for us, in our place. Thus they have to be accepted as ours. Or rather, our true body and blood are now the body and blood of Jesus Christ who has taken our place. We are strong, therefore, as the man in Christ grows up in us, as we put off the old life and put on the new. And our feeding upon the

11. Cf. John 6:31ff.
12. Cf. John 6:51, 53ff.

bread and wine brings this truth concretely before us, and by its witness furthers the response of penitence, faith and obedience in which this growth and renewal take place.

The thought of sustenance is also closely linked with that of fellowship, which is, of course, plainly brought out in the action itself by the fact that the Supper is not a private meal but a public partaking of the bread and wine around the one table.[13] This aspect of fellowship is so important that it has found expression in one of the common titles for the sacrament, the Holy Communion. But here again, we must be careful not to give to the fellowship a generalized or sentimentalized significance. This is not just ordinary fellowship. It is not just a kind of variant of the club dinner or social evening. And the pity is that so many churches seem to feel it necessary to revert to the worldly version of conviviality to foster fellowship within themselves, when all the time they are called to a deeper level of communion than can ever be afforded by social occasions, however pleasant and in their own way justifiable. No, this is not just any fellowship; it is holy or sacred fellowship. It is fellowship at the very deepest level and in the most radical way. We must now try to see what is meant by this fellowship.

In the first place, it is fellowship in and with the Lord Himself.[14] This is suggested in two ways. First, the Lord Himself is the true Host at His table, as He is the ultimate Minister of baptism. But second, as we have seen, we are pointed to His body and blood as our true life and sustenance, and therefore we are brought into, or fostered in, a living relationship with Himself. It is not merely that the Lord is present according to His promise that where two or three gather in His name He is in the midst.[15] It is not merely that by the Spirit we are transported back, as it were, to Calvary and upward to the right hand of the Father. But the One with whom we have fellowship is the One who took our flesh, and in our flesh took our place, dying to sin, and bearing away in His body the sinful body of what we are in ourselves. And He is also the One who in our flesh was raised again the third day from the dead, that His risen life

13. I Cor. 10:16.
14. I John 1:3.
15. Matt. 18:20.

might be our true life, the new man which we are in Him, for the moment by faith, but one day and for ever in reality and fullness. Hence, when we participate in the bread and wine at the Lord's invitation and in His presence by the Spirit, the fellowship with the Lord which is attested and fostered is the vital fellowship in which, as Paul says, we are members of His body, and one spirit with Him.[16]

But, secondly, our fellowship is with one another.[17] This is also suggested in two ways. As already indicated, this second sacrament is essentially an affair of the whole church. The same is true of baptism, yet we can rightly speak of "my" baptism. To talk of "my" supper, however, as in the dreadful phrase "making my communion," is quite intolerable, even though the personal aspect is given its place in the fact that each must receive for himself. The fact is that this is something which we do together. Nor is it merely that we meet with a common purpose, around a common table, and in response to a common invitation. Rather, we do so as the members of a family, as the company of those who confess Jesus Christ, as those who have the mark of our new birth in baptism, as believers in the one Savior, children of the one Father, and recipients of the one Spirit.

But this leads us to the further thought that we have fellowship one with another because we all have that living fellowship with Jesus Christ Himself. In other words, we take the same bread and drink of the same cup.[18] We are members of the one body of Christ and therefore we are radically and unavoidably members of one another. Even as sinners we are united in the one body and blood of Jesus Christ to which the bread and wine bear witness. For this One has taken the place of the many. He has died for all, and therefore all are dead in Him.[19] The many sinners with all their differences and divisions and suspicions and hostilities have a common meeting-place on the cross of Golgotha, or rather in the One who was done to death on that cross. And if there is this unity of sinners in the crucified body of Jesus, how much more so is there the unity of believers in

16. I Cor. 6:15,17.
17. I John 1:3.
18. I Cor. 10:14.
19. II Cor. 5:14.

the risen and ascended body of Jesus Christ. For now we all have our common life, our new life in faith, in the One who was raised for our justification. Our true life, indeed our only genuine life, is now in Him. It cannot, then, be an isolated or divided life. It cannot be a life in which we can go our different ways or be engaged in mutual indifference or enmity. It can only be a life, not merely in comradeship, but in vital communion. And this communion is attested and fostered by the fact that we eat of the one loaf and drink of the one cup.

For this reason and in this sense the Lord's Supper, no less and perhaps even more than baptism, is a sacrament of Christian unity. To be sure, it is administered continually, so that there can be no question of the common acceptance of a once-for-all administration. Yet the Bible tells us that, as there is one baptism, so there is one loaf and one cup.[20] For there are not two or more Christs, nor two or more Calvaries. The body and blood were only this body and blood of Jesus Christ, and they were offered up only this once. Hence, though there may be many administrations even at the same time and at the same place (through pressure of numbers), there cannot and ought not to be opposing, competitive, or divided tables, or suppers of the Lord.

As a sacrament of fellowship in the one body of Christ, the Lord's Supper is naturally a call to individual Christians that they should come to the Lord's Table in brotherly harmony.[21] It is not a mere warning that they should stay away if not in harmony, although to come to this sacrament when one is knowingly unforgiving or unloving in relation to another is a dreadful denial of everything that the action proclaims. Nor is it an excuse for separating from Christians with whom we are at odds and going to a different communion, for God is not mocked by an evasion which is tantamount to the establishment of two loaves and two cups, and therefore again a denial of our basic oneness in Christ. On the contrary, it is a summons to make up the differences, to confess that we are all sinners crucified in the one body of Christ, and all believers having our new and true life in His one risen body. Rightly used under the Holy Spirit, the

20. I Cor. 10:16,17.
21. 1 Cor. 11:17ff.

Lord's Supper offers a continuing opportunity for the lesser reconciliations with our fellows on the basis and within the context of the great reconciliation accomplished on our behalf in Jesus Christ. In this sense it is both a sign and an instrument of unity between individuals.

But the Lord's Supper is also a call to communities of Christians, to different denominations or churches, to a realization and an expression of their basic unity in Jesus Christ.[22] For after all, in general as in its individual members the Church is basically and essentially one in the crucified and risen body of Jesus Christ. And the corresponding loaf and cup not only declare this fact, but they are a challenge and means to its practical outworking.

There are two implications in the relationships of churches. First, there can be no denial of communion to visiting members of other churches who have made a profession of faith in Jesus Christ. To fence the table in the interests of members who might come without proper self-examination is one thing;[23] to fence it against those whom we presume not to regard as genuine or orderly Christians because of some difference of belief or defect in ecclesiastical structure is quite another. The former can be an instrument of real fellowship; the latter is a blatant denial of fellowship. Naturally, church members are not to be encouraged to wander from one table to another, for normally their place is with their brethren in the congregation to which they belong. Again, demonstrations of intercommunion are not to be commended, for they entail what is almost a misuse, or at least a truncated application of the sacrament. But the fact remains that free intercommunion is surely demanded by the very nature and message of the sacrament where circumstances justify it.

Is this not enough? Many who claim to be Reformed would think so. But the fact is that the Reformers themselves, building on the Bible, saw a second implication as well. This is that the church must be united in the one locality[24] and therefore that there must be the most serious effort to avoid or to end denominationalism. Even with the freest inter-

22. Cf. I Cor. 11:18.
23. Cf. I Cor. 11:28.
24. I Cor. 11:20.

communion, the one body is not fully expressed if there are rival administrations. Mere weight of numbers demands that there should be many congregations, even in the one place. But these are not, or are not meant to be, competitive bodies. They are not separated as denominational churches in the one locality are separated. Their loaf and cup are still one. Denominationalism, however, establishes two or three or innumerable loaves and cups which jostle with one another and from which we may even come to imagine that we have liberty to choose. That the loaf and cup must be one, that the new and true reality of Christians is life in the one body of Christ, demands that the old, sinful, defeated and outdated reality of schism should be averted or healed as far as possible. The churches are to become and be what they are in Christ. The Lord's Supper with its one loaf and one cup is a condemnation of their present structure with its many loaves and many cups, and a call to the reformation under the Word of God, or the conformation to the mind and body of Christ, which will not mean the end of the congregations and therefore of diversity and richness, but will certainly involve the end of the kind of division against which we are warned already by Paul's answer to incipient denominationalism in Corinth.[25]

The fact that the sacrament so vividly and intransigeantly brings before us the body and blood of Christ, given or offered up for us, as we see even in relation to its lessons of nourishment, fellowship, and unity, means that the thought of sacrifice is prominent in the action. In relation to the sacrifice of Christ, it is naturally a remembrance of the once-for-all event of Calvary, when "a full, perfect, and sufficient sacrifice, oblation, and satisfaction" was made "for the sins of the whole world." But, as in the case of baptism, there goes with the remembrance of this offering the thought of our responsive action which takes an analogous form. In other words, answering to the sacrifice of Christ, there is the offering which we can and do take to Him. And the Lord's Supper has the further significance that it is itself an expression of this offering, and that it summons us to its practical realization in our future life and service.

25. I Cor. 1:10ff.

In the first instance, as is most proper, it is an offering of thanksgiving and praise,[26] for the true response to the grace of God is surely gratitude. We best respond to the love of God by receiving what He has done for us and praising Him for it. This aspect has always been prominent. It is contained, indeed, in the action itself, for when the Lord took bread, and later the cup, He gave thanks;[27] and if we have cause to thank God even for the earthly elements with their physical sustenance, how much greater cause we have to thank Him for that which they represent, the body of Christ broken for us and the blood outpoured! It was in recognition of this element that the term Eucharist came into usage as a title for the sacrament, and though not so comprehensive as the Lord's Supper, it is a good and meaningful alternative (unlike the medieval and Romanist mass). Among the Reformers, Zwingli liked to think of the Supper as a thanksgiving, and in the Anglican service, in addition to the action of thanksgiving, the words of administration contain the phrase "Be ye thankful," and the closing prayer asks that God will accept this sacrifice of praise and thanksgiving. In acceptance and recognition of God's gracious offering of Himself for us, we bring to Him the offering of our adoring gratitude, not merely in the words we utter, but in the very action of receiving that which He has done.

But acceptance of what Christ has done for us, as we have seen already from baptism, means a corresponding action of self-denial and renewal, and therefore the Lord's Supper is a further and continuing call that we should genuinely offer ourselves to Jesus Christ, ceasing to live to ourselves, for our own ends and purposes and pleasure, and living wholly to the Lord, in His service and according to His will. In other words, as we see that Christ has offered Himself for us, in grateful response we are summoned to offer ourselves to Him, presenting our bodies as living sacrifices, holy and acceptable to God, which is our reasonable service.[28]

In this connection, it is perhaps worth noting that in the Reformation view it is a mistake to identify this offering too closely with the offertory, or especially with the provision of

26. Heb. 13:15.
27. Matt. 26:26; Luke 22:19.
28. Rom. 12:1.

the elements of bread and wine. The latter thought is particularly unfortunate, for while it is true that the Savior comes of our human stock — and this must be emphasized — the chief thing about His atonement is that it is God Himself who provides the Lamb for the sacrifice.[29] The offering of alms is naturally a part of the self-giving which is demanded of us in response to the love of Christ so graphically portrayed to us.[30] And it is a matter for surprise that there should be some who can more or less regularly partake of the sacrament and not be stirred by the total self-giving of God to shame at their own lack of generosity in support of the church and its world-wide mission. But the responsive self-giving of the Christian goes far beyond this. The sacrifice required of us is the total dedication of our very life and being and powers and time and energies and purposes, all that we have and are, to the God to whom we now belong because we have been bought with the precious blood of Jesus Christ,[31] because our old life is now over and our new and true and only life is the life which we have in Him.

Along these lines, the sacrament has some very challenging things to say to those who are prepared to receive it obediently and prayerfully, and within the context of the Gospel and its summons. Sometimes, as we have seen, it may be a call to the first giving of ourselves to Jesus Christ in repentance and faith. Always, it will be a call to the laying of our old aims and desires and impulses and ambitions and achievements and follies at the feet of Jesus Christ and the acceptance of His new powers and purposes. Always it will be a call to the offering of ourselves in some form of service and witness, that we may give others to eat of the bread of life,[32] the true bread which comes down from heaven.[33] And within the wider sphere of service it may sometimes carry with it the special vocation to the ministry of word and sacrament at home or overseas, the tremendous reality of the sending of the Son in grace finding its response in the grateful cry of the servant: "Lord, here am I, send me."[34] In sum, to partake

29. John 1:29.
30. Heb. 13:16.
31. I Cor. 6:20.
32. Luke 9:13.
33. John 6:33.
34. Is. 6:8.

of the sacrament in genuine remembrance of what Christ has
done for us is an invitation, a permission, and a command
to do what we can for Him, not as independent agents, but
as vessels fit and ready for the Master's use.

There is just one final aspect. In the account of the institution of the Lord's Supper in St. Luke's Gospel there is a
saying of Jesus that He "will not drink of the fruit of the
vine, until the kingdom of God shall come,"[35] and a further
saying that the disciples shall "eat and drink at my table in
my kingdom."[36] In something of the same connection, although along different lines, we read in I Corinthians that
the sacrament is a shewing of the Lord's death "till he
come."[37] From the very outset, therefore, this sacrament, no
less than baptism, has had a forward as well as a backward
look. It is a reminder that the Lord who died and rose again
will also return in glory to consummate His work. It is an
action for the time between the ascension and the second
advent, when Jesus Christ is no longer present in the flesh,
but in word and sacrament is with His people by the Spirit.
It is a pointer to the Messianic banquet when the Lord will
be the Host at His heavenly table and many shall come
from east and west and north and south to sit and feast
with Him.[38] It is a witness that we are not to labor for the
meat which perishes,[39] but to realize that our true aim is to
nourish the eternal life which in Jesus Christ is already by
faith our new and true life, and which can be daily renewed,
even though the outward man perish.[40] It is perhaps even a
sign, through the use of material means of sustenance, that
both body and soul will have their place in the final redemption, so that by the body and blood of Christ both must be
preserved to eternal life.

In this respect the sacrament adds its witness to that of
the word. It sets the life of the Christian in an eschatological
perspective. It keeps before him the goal to which he moves
as well as the source from which he comes. It is the food of

35. Luke 22:18.
36. Luke 22:30.
37. I Cor. 11:26.
38. Luke 13:29.
39. John 6:24.
40. II Cor. 4:16.

IN THE REFORMATION CHURCHES

the pilgrim on the march, not of the settled inhabitant.[41] It calls him from a life oriented to this age, which was condemned and destroyed at the cross, and summons him to look forward in hope and expectation for the kingdom which has come, but the coming of which has yet to be consummated and revealed. The purpose of Holy Communion is not merely that we should be strengthened in faith and deepened in love; it is also that we should be nurtured in hope.

This witness has, of course, its solemn side. It rebukes us for our worldliness, in respect to wealth and property no less than fame or pleasure. It exposes the hollowness of our pretended consecration and service. It tells us that we must give account of our stewardship[42] and that every secret thought and word and work will be disclosed.[43] It shows us what kind of people we must be as believers and servants awaiting their Lord's return.[44] But while all this is true and important, the final note is surely one of joy. We are not hopeless, dispirited, terrified, or bewildered pilgrims. As liberated exiles on the way home, we look for the King Himself to greet us in the manifestation of His triumph and fulfillment of His rule. Setting our life in this large and glorious perspective, the sacrament puts on our lips a song, not merely of praise and thanksgiving, but of triumphant expectation.[45] And to the promise of His coming, it teaches us response, not of weariness and despair, but of vibrant expectancy: "Even so, come, Lord Jesus."[46]

41. Heb. 13:14, I Pet. 2:11.
42. Matt. 24:42ff.
43. I Cor. 4:5.
44. II Pet. 3:11.
45. Luke 21:28.
46. Rev. 22:20.

CHAPTER SIX

THE ADMINISTRATION
OF THE LORD'S SUPPER

THE SECOND SACRAMENT, like the first, consists of an action which is extremely simple. Bread is taken and broken, with blessing or thanksgiving, and then distributed and eaten. A cup of wine is handed round after the appropriate blessing. And normally the circumstances of the institution are recalled, the two accompanying formulae, "This is my body . . ." and "This is my blood," being particularly recited.[1] Again, however, this simple action can be performed in a variety of ways and with many different additions or accompaniments. We shall now try to see what shape it normally takes in the Reformation churches as they try to bring their administration into the closest possible conformity with Holy Scripture.

A first question concerns the elements used in the sacrament. Since bread and wine are quite generally available, the question of permissible substitutes does not arise in Reformation theology. Bread is taken in the usual sense. It is not thought necessary, therefore, that a special form of unleavened bread or wafer should be used for this purpose. In honor of the occasion, it is suitable that the best possible quality of bread should be used, but this is not essential, since what finally matters is the use to which it is put rather than the element itself.

Wine, again, is construed in the customary sense, but there is no fussy argument about fermentation. The question of unfermented "wine" would hardly arise in the Reforma-

1. 1 Cor. 11:24ff.

tion period, but it is alien to the Reformed outlook to be
scrupulously legal in matters of this kind. On the other hand,
the practice of adding water to the wine, presumably to
denote the mingled water and blood which flowed from the
side of the Crucified,[2] is not recommended since there is no
warrant for it in the institution.

A more serious question which arose in relation to the
wine was the medieval practice of forbidding the cup to the
laity. The reason advanced for this, that it prevented the
possible profanation of spilling the wine, was not regarded
as sufficient by the Reformers. Apart from this, the prohibition was obviously of recent date, and plainly contrary to
the obvious institution and command of Scripture. An important principle is at stake in this connection, for it cannot
be conceded that the church has any power to make rules
contrary to the plain directions of the Bible. All the Reformation churches agree in this, even those which, like the
Lutheran and Anglican, allow the church a power to au-
thorize rites for which there is no direct biblical sanction.
It is perhaps worth noting that many of the traditionalists,
too, were uneasy on this point.

Integral to the action of the second there is, of course, a
form of blessing or thanksgiving,[3] and around this there
cluster many of the controversies in relation to the Lord's
Supper. In the medieval church the prayer of blessing had
come to be thought of very distinctly as a prayer of "consecration" and linked with the supposed "real" presence of
Christ on the one side and eucharistic offering on the other.
Naturally, the Reformed churches preserve a prayer of blessing. But they purge it of its superstitious or erroneous
elements. It becomes primarily a prayer of remembrance,
recalling the event of the institution, attesting the death of
Jesus Christ to which we are pointed by the elements, and
giving thanks to God for His gracious action and the benefits
which it has secured for us. If the thought of consecration
remains at all, it is merely as a setting aside of these common
elements for the particular purpose of the sacrament. In this
connection, a form of invocation of the Holy Spirit is not
altogether impermissible, for although this is not specifically

2. John 19:34.
3. Matt. 26:26ff.

commanded by the Bible, it is in accordance with the general usage of Scripture that in the use of the means of grace there should be prayer to the Lord of these means by whom alone Christ is now present to us. If this is retained, however, care must be taken to see that it is not linked with a mistaken view of the eucharistic presence and work.

It is no less essential that the elements should be taken and consumed than that there should be the prayer of blessing or thanksgiving.[4] Otherwise the action is not fully performed and there is no true sacrament. This being the case, the practice of setting elements aside in a special place, and making them the object of acts of adoration either in the church or in public processions, is obviously contrary to the whole nature and point of Holy Communion. Originally, the practice seems to have grown out of a desire that the sick should share the same bread and wine as those able to attend the service, and there can hardly be any objection to this custom in itself. But with the passage of time it came to be associated with so much that is dubious that the Reformed churches think it better not even to attempt to restore the earlier custom, but to discontinue all forms of reservation.

The fact that by nature the Lord's Supper is a meal and not a sacrifice means that it is properly administered at a table and not an altar. In a loose sense, as in many of the fathers, the table of the Lord may perhaps be called an "altar" in recollection of the one sacrifice for sin made by the Lord of the table. But there are serious objections to this course. In the first place, there are pagan associations which are necessarily unhelpful. In the second, there is the danger of coming to think of the sacrament itself as in some sense a repetition of the sacrifice which it attests. And third, it is almost impossible to make clear the necessary distinctions to those who do not have the requisite theological training. In these circumstances, the Refomed churches think it better to abandon a word which does not properly belong to the context of the Supper, and wooden tables are used in place of the stone altars so common in the medieval church. Simple appointments and furnishings are also thought to be more in keeping with the original institution.

4. Matt. 26:26.

The action of eating and drinking presupposes that there are recipients, as at the original institution. This might almost seem to be self-evident, but again the medieval church had succeeded in perverting even so basic an aspect of the sacrament. This had happened in two ways. In the first place, there had grown up the practice of solitary masses, i.e., administrations at which no one was present at all except the minister. The practice is so obviously corrupt and pointless that one may be tempted to ask how it could possibly have arisen at all. But the solitary mass is an essential part of the whole system of atonement or retribution which arises out of the misunderstanding of baptism and its meaning. These masses are supposed to procure grace for the living or dead for whom they are said or "offered," and the endowment of masses means that there are many priests who must spend quite a considerable portion of their time in working through the necessary programme. Naturally, the Reformers were able to go to the very root of this error, but quite apart from the false teaching which explains its origin, it is an obvious abuse of the sacrament for which there can be no place in Reformation churches. Even for reasons of personal piety or edification, ministers must not administer communion simply to themselves, for without a congregation there is no communion.

But secondly, and in connection with much the same group of errors, there had grown up the practice of non-communicating attendance at mass. The strange paradox of the Roman church is that mass is the most important service, and on some days an absolute obligation, yet it is depreciated in fact by being turned into something other than the original Supper. The people are almost forced to attend, yet they are not encouraged to participate except at infrequent intervals. Something different — an alleged miracle and offering — has replaced the original means of grace, and therefore the latter is no longer essential. This practice is sometimes excused on the ground that communicating is so holy a matter that it should be undertaken only on special occasions and with special preparation. But, in effect, non-communicating attendance is a perversion of the original action which can only have the most unhappy consequences, teaching a way which is different from the Gospel, closing the true sacrament to those for whose benefit it was instituted, and thus hampering its operation.

It is worth noting that the custom of infrequent attendance at Holy Communion was so well established at the time of the Reformation that the Reformers were unable to overcome it. The general view of the Reformers was that, considering scriptural precedent and the purpose and meaning of the sacrament, it ought to be administered each week, or monthly at the very least. But this proved to be incapable of realization, and the most that could be attempted was a quarterly communion. The Church of England maintained a weekly ante-communion, but could not insist on more than three communions a year as a rule of membership; and it is interesting to note that even today, when weekly communions are fairly common in the Anglican communion, the bulk of communicant members will not attend except at Christmas and Easter. In its own way a well-attended communion at infrequent intervals is, of course, most impressive, but there can be little doubt that it falls short of the true use of the sacrament, which ought to take the form of well-attended communions at frequent intervals.

Another relic of non-communicating attendance is perhaps to be found in the excessive fencing of the table which has sometimes prevailed in Reformed circles. The sacrament is a solemn matter, and should certainly be approached with genuine reverence and sincerity. But matters are carried too far when it is regarded with such awe that it is hardly ever received at all. The point is that, like all the means of grace, the Lord's Supper is ordained for the use and benefit of sinners. If we wait until we are worthy to receive, we shall never receive at all. We receive the sacrament of Christ's body and blood as we receive the Lord Himself, coming just as we are, confessing our unworthiness, and looking to Him for forgiveness and righteousness. Thus, for all its show of reverence, fear of reception is contrary to the genuine teaching and practice of the Reformation.

At the same time it is obvious that there must be certain rules for the right reception of the Lord's Supper. For instance, it is essential that the recipient should be baptized, and that he should also have made a personal confession of faith if baptized in infancy. This is the obvious purpose behind the Anglican rubric that only those who have been confirmed should be admitted to the Lord's table. In the Church of England confirmation is the service at which personal profession of faith is made, and therefore within the church those who are not willing or ready to make such a confession cannot be admitted as adult members to Holy Communion. There is no implied exclusion of others in sister-churches who have made their profession of faith in some other form; and it is not insisted that the confirmation be episcopal, though this is the domestic practice in the Anglican communion. The main point is that profession must precede communion.

Again, it is obviously improper that Christians should come to communion if they are willfully unrepentant in respect to certain sins, especially in their relations with fellow-Christians.[5] It is for this reason that there is usually some form of preparation which involves the opportunity for self-examination and confession; and that the ministers, elders, or churchwardens may have the right to forbid communion to those who are flagrantly sinful and impenitent, not in a spirit of censoriousness, but to prevent them from hypocrisy and to summon them to repentance. This is the legitimate form of fencing the tables, but it must not be carried to the extreme point of a legalistic discipline which hampers the functioning of the Lord's Supper as a sacrament of grace. Fasting communion is not enjoined, as this is so obviously related to a false understanding of the sacrament.

Again, there can be no doubt that all Christians ought to attend Holy Communion with some measure of frequency. If they do not, it is a sign both of indifference to the saving action which is signified and of withdrawal from fellowship with the brethren. For this reason, a minimum attendance at the sacrament is regarded as a test of membership. But again the Gospel must not be transformed into Law. If a legitimate requirement is interpreted and applied as a rigorous regulation, it encourages formal attendance on the one side and perhaps discourages the sincere return of the lapsed on the other. The demand for attendance may and must be made, but it is to be made in the form of a gracious invitation and permission rather than a legal enactment.

5. 1 Cor. 11:27ff.

The action presupposes a minister as well as recipients, and a few words may be said about this aspect of the matter. It has always been recognized in the church that no one ought to administer Holy Communion without proper authorization. Since the sacrament has never been regarded as so absolutely necessary as baptism, no exceptions have been made to this rule. The Reformation churches agree that while there might be exceptional circumstances as in the case of castaways, the minister alone should be in charge of the administration, though he may be assisted by elders in the distribution. They naturally do not accept the view that in the strict sense only a bishop has plenary authority to administer the word and sacraments, and that other ministers may not do so except by delegation; though even the medieval and Romanist theologians did not go to this extreme. Nor can they agree that episcopal ordination is essential to a valid ministry. This form of ordination may or may not be retained, as decided by individual churches. The true minister, however, is the one who is inwardly called by God and outwardly set aside by the congregation for his work, as clearly stated in the various Reformed confessions (including the Anglican). He, and he alone, has the task of administering the means of grace to the people.

It is emphasized, however, that the minister does not in any sense act as a sacrificing priest, or a mediator between God and the people. Christ is the one Mediator[6] and the great Highpriest,[7] and now that He has offered Himself there is no further need of sacrifice. The minister acts as the servant of Christ and of the people, and it is in token of this genuine "ministry" that he stands either behind or alongside the table, and not before the altar as in the medieval and Roman church. In this connection it may be noted that the widespread Anglican reversion to another usage is in plain defiance of the rubrical direction and no less evident contradiction of the doctrinal presuppositions of the service.

In the actual conduct of the service, the Reformation churches stress again the need for the ordinary language of the people. A foreign tongue may increase the sense of

6. I Tim. 2:5.
7. Heb. 4:15, 5:1ff.

mystery and even in some circumstances of reverence. But
the mystery and reverence promoted in this way are those of
superstition. The mystery of the Gospel is a revealed mystery, and the reverence associated with the work of Christ a
reverence based upon understanding. The same holds good
of the actions performed, especially in relation to the blessing of the elements. No false mystery is to be suggested by
concealed and secretive movements which in the end can
only resemble the mumbo-jumbo of heathendom or the
sleight of a conjuror. The simple movements carry their own
mystery and dignity, and all that is needed is their reverent
and open performance in obedience with the institution
and command.

As in the case of baptism, it is thought necessary that
Holy Communion should be brought into direct relationship
with the word. The sacrament as a visible word needs the
audible word to declare its meaning and to make explicit its
summons. Thus the service of Communion will include not
merely a reading of the account of the original institution,
but also other Scriptures, exhortation, and preaching.[8] The
inveterate tendency in some circles to divorce the sacrament
from the word, or at least from the living word in the form
of preaching and translated Scripture, is an obvious indica-
tion that the real meaning, purpose, and power of the
sacrament are not yet perceived.

In addition to the reading of Scripture and preaching, the
Reformed churches agree that the service of Holy Communion should include the praise of God, prayers of penitence,
intercession and thanksgiving, and an offertory. The praise
of God is particularly suitable in a sacrifice of praise and
thanksgiving, and seems in any case to have scriptural precedent in the hymn sung by the disciples at the Last Supper.[9]
Penitential prayer forms a fitting preparation for the worthy
reception of the elements, replacing the penance demanded
in Roman practice. Intercession is always required of the
Christian,[10] and thanksgiving is fitly offered not merely for
the means of grace, but for the grace itself, the Lord Jesus
Christ and all the benefits which He has procured by His

8. Cf. the Johannine discourses at the institution.
9. Matt. 26:30.
10. I Tim. 2:1ff.

death and passion. Finally, the offertory provides an opportunity for the concrete and practical expression of the response of self-sacrifice evoked by the broken body and outpoured blood of Christ.

While the Reformation churches appreciate the value and necessity of an orderly and dignified administration, they do not favor the elaborate ceremonial which from early days has grouped itself around this as other actions.[11] Sacrificial vestments are obviously due to a misunderstanding of the nature of the sacrament, and are thus to be discarded with altars, or for that matter, the word *priest* (which is retained in the Church of England only as a contraction of presbyter and not in the sense of a sacrificing priest). Candles may at one time been useful as illumination, but now that they have been superseded by more efficient modes of lighting there is no point in clinging to them for their supposed religious or mystical value. Incense, too, had its own part in the worship of Old Testament days, when there was a special altar of incense, but now that the detailed ceremonies of the Law have been fulfilled in Christ there is no point in trying to perpetuate them. Actions like the kissing of the book, the washing of hands, and the ringing of bells, and stylized postures on the part of the celebrant, all belong to the complex of a false interpretation and appreciation of the Lord's Supper, and are thus discontinued. The term *mass* is also abandoned for much the same reason. It carries no intrinsic meaning, and is thus necessarily colored by its associations. In accordance with its institution it is recognized that the Supper may be administered in the afternoon or evening as well as the morning, though there is of course no binding law in the matter.

Another point worth noting is that in the intercessions rightly included in the service good care is taken to break the misleading connection of Holy Communion with purgatory. The ancient form had found a place not only for prayers for the dead, but also for the invocation of saints. Neither of these is essential when it is seen that Christ Himself is an all-sufficient Mediator and Advocate, and that therefore the emphasis in the prayers of Reformation orders,

11. The Lutherans are an exception, but they explicitly deprive the ceremonial of doctrinal significance.

whether prescribed or free, is upon the fullness and power of the work that Christ Himself has done. The Reformation churches do not condemn in principle a liturgical form, as the extremer Puritans and Independents may lead us to suppose. This is a matter which the churches may decide for themselves, so long as what is done is not contrary to Scripture. But on the Reformed side the general tendency is in favor of a directory rather than a fixed liturgy, i.e., the suggesting of a general pattern within which the minister may exercise his own liberty. In any case, however, the traditional forms of prayer are so closely linked with erroneous doctrine that they cannot be taken into the Reformation service without the most drastic alteration.

In the actual distribution the common practice of Reformed churches is for the people to receive the elements in their own places, namely, in the pews. This is thought to be most in accord with the original institution and also most conducive to quiet reflection. In this, as in many other matters, the more conservative Church of England is an exception. For one thing, it preserves kneeling at the reception of the elements, not in token of adoration of the bread and wine, but as a more reverent attitude. To the argument that the disciples did not kneel, it is pointed out that in all probability they did not sit either, but reclined. Again, although distribution was first made in the body of the church, from the time of Laud the people have been directed to come in orderly fashion to the table itself for reception. In some ways this is perhaps a mistake, for although reception in this way is not without its own impressiveness, the movement breaks the stillness at the decisive moment. A further point is that the distribution is concentrated in the hands of the minister or ministers; indeed, it is because of this that coming up to the table makes for greater ease and order in the Anglican service. But while it is good Reformed doctrine that only the minister should dispense the word and sacraments, it is not absolutely necessary that each communicant should receive the bread and wine directly at his hands. All the Reformed churches agree that each person should take the bread and wine for himself, and not have the bread thrust on his tongue or the wine tilted into his mouth.

In normal circumstances, the Reformation churches insist that communicants should receive the sacrament at their own churches. This does not exclude individual visits to other churches when away from home, but it is definitely meant to prohibit the shifting from church to church which is one of the unsatisfactory features of modern independency or individualism. Neither discipline, fellowship, nor genuine edification is possible where members of a church are migratory. For the true Reformation Christian, the individual congregation is the church, not in competition with neighboring congregations, but also not in confusion with them. If aspects of the congregation are wrong, or the services are not found to be so inspiring or helpful as elsewhere, the task of the member is to contribute to amendment rather than to disclaim responsibility and seek his private ends in some other quarter. Rightly understood, a loyalty to the congregation is a loyalty to the larger territorial church, and ultimately to the church universal; and this loyalty is best expressed and served by normal communion at one's own church. In special cases, more common today when there is so much more movement, the Reformation churches recommend and practice free intercommunion both within and among ourselves.

Linked with this emphasis upon church loyalty is the doctrine that the grace of the sacrament is not dependent upon the gifts or even the character of the minister. This has been perceived from a very early date in the church. Augustine, for example, pointed out that the baptism or healings performed by Judas were no less valid and efficacious than those performed by John or Peter. It is naturally to be recommended that the minister should be as able and upright as possible, and the Reformation churches have always set a high standard for the ministry. But the true minister of the sacrament is Jesus Christ Himself by the Holy Spirit, and therefore the fact that a neighboring church has a minister who has greater gifts of speech or personality, or a more impressive form of service, is no reason to abandon one's own communion in the hope of greater spiritual benefits. The latter course betrays not only a selfish individualism, but a rationalizing of the operation of the sacrament which is neither biblical nor Reformed.

In conclusion, however, it must be emphasized that the fact that the validity and power of the sacrament are not dependent on the gifts or character of the minister does not mean that it is automatic in operation. Christ is proffered to all with His gifts and graces, but He is received only by those who came in penitence and faith. Hence, the demand is made, both in the invitation to communion and in the service itself, that those who come to the Lord's table should do so, not with a sense of their own worthiness which could only mean a final hypocrisy and unbelief, but in full acknowledgment of their sinfulness and whole-hearted reliance upon Jesus Christ and His work. These are simple but deep requirements which cannot be enforced legalistically but must always be kept to the forefront when the sacrament is administered. For even though the administration itself be as correct, as scriptural, or as effective as possible, it will necessarily fail of its true purpose and effect unless it is received with penitence and faith, and thus confirms and strengthens the response of the recipient.

CHAPTER SEVEN

THE REAL PRESENCE

————————

THE LORD'S SUPPER no less than baptism has been the theme of a good deal of misunderstanding and controversy in spite of the simplicity of the action and the basic clarity of its meaning. In the main, these errors have centered upon two related questions, that of the presence of Christ in the sacrament, and that of the relationship of the sacrament to His self-offering on the cross. Once the initial battles concerning justification and Scripture had been fought, these eucharistic questions emerged as the dominant issues of the Reformation. To us today, they may sometimes appear to be remote. But we do well to remember that it was primarily for their stand of these doctrines that men like Cranmer and Ridley in England were burned as heretics, and that the teaching which they opposed is still the official and binding doctrine of the papal church.

It has always been accepted, and the Reformation churches do not dispute the fact, that Christ Himself is present where the word is preached and the sacraments of the Gospel are administered. He has given us the definite promise of His presence where two or three gather in His name,[1] and there is also the general promise that He is with His people always, even to the end of the world.[2] But the question which arises is whether there is a special presence in the administration of Holy Communion, or more generally, what is the nature of this presence of Christ.

The idea of a special presence in this sacrament arises mainly from the statements of Christ Himself in the upper

1. Matt. 18:20.
2. Matt. 28:20.

room when He identifies the bread with His body and the cup of wine with His blood.[3] In the early church it was not unnaturally taken that the broken bread and outpoured wine are distributed in order to give us a concrete sense of the body and blood of Christ given up to death for our salvation. In the common fashion of sacramental exposition allowed and used by the Reformers, the sign is spoken of in terms of the thing signified, and *vice versa*. The true reality of the sacrament is not the giving and eating of bread and wine, but the self-offering and receiving of Christ; and the external elements serve to attest this internal reality.

So long as no attempt was made at closer explanation or definition, all was well. More vividly, perhaps, than baptism, this sacrament brings home to us the incarnation of Christ and His death in the body, so that Christ is proffered to us with all His saving benefits. The trouble arose in the Middle Ages when a theoretical exposition of the relationship between sign and thing signified was attempted. Even then, all might have been well, for those who find it helpful to interpret Christian truth in terms of current philosophy may perhaps be allowed to do so individually under the overriding authority of Scripture. But unfortunately the medieval church took the serious step, only two hundred years before the Reformation, of making this interpretation an authoritative dogma necessary to eternal salvation. It was this audacious and unfounded innovation which made the question of the presence so decisive an issue.

There can be no doubt, as we have said, that when Christ takes the bread He speaks of it in terms of His body, and that when He takes the cup He speaks of it in terms of His blood. But are we to conclude from this that in the Lord's Supper there is a special presence of Christ in body and blood, i.e., a corporal presence, such as we are not to expect in the preaching of the word or the administration of baptism? This is the claim of the medievalists, and against the obvious objection that the body and blood of Christ cannot be seen or touched the following explanation is advanced within the framework of the realistic philosophy of the time.

In every object we have to reckon, not merely with the variable external features perceptible to the senses, the so-

3. Matt. 26:26,28.

called "accidents," but also with the "real" and abiding thing itself, the so-called "substance." Thus a table may be high or low, round, square or oblong, wooden or metal, one-legged or four-legged, smooth or rough, but for all the possible variety of accidents it is still a table. There is a true and ultimate reality of table independent of the accidents.

Now when we have to do with Holy Communion it is evident that the accidents are those of bread and wine. This cannot be gainsaid, for it is plainly attested by our senses. But since Christ said that the bread and wine taken in Communion are His body and blood, there must also be a sense in which the body and blood of Christ are truly present. The distinction between accidents and substance provides the clue to something which would otherwise be a sheer impossibility. By the miraculous operation of God, the substance of bread and wine is replaced by that of the body and blood of Christ, present now under the accidents of the material elements. This is transubstantiation, the change of the one substance into the other. And it gives us a real presence of Christ, the presence of the very substance of His body and blood, such as we do not have in other cases.

There are two main arguments in favor of this view. The first is that according to the statement of Christ the bread and wine are the body and blood of Christ,[4] and therefore in some way this must be the case. The other is that, although this change of substance is a miracle, it is not an impossibility with God,[5] and is thus to be accepted as the only explanation of what takes place.

The doctrine has, of course, many ramifications in the whole medieval scheme of faith and practice. If Christ is present in this specific form, it is obvious that the Lord's Supper is the supreme act of devotion, that it consists essentially in an act of adoration, that the elements must be treated with particular respect and may even serve as a focus of worship, that all who take communion receive the actual substance of Christ's body and blood whether they receive in faith or not, and that the moment of consecration, when the miracle takes place, is one of peculiar sanctity, the minister himself being an agent of the miraculous power of God and

4. Matt. 26:26,28.
5. Luke 1:37.

therefore of extraordinary distinction and authority. The detailed outworking of these thoughts need not concern us in this contest, but it will surely be seen that this doctrine is the copestone, though not perhaps the foundation, of the whole of the medieval fabric. Its bearing on the question of the eucharistic sacrifice will call for separate and more detailed consideration.

The Reformers were unanimous in regarding this whole doctrine as a perversion of the Gospel, and apart from Luther and his followers, who were impressed by the emphatic statements of Christ, they could not agree that there is in Communion any substantial or localized presence of Christ's body and blood, and therefore any form of a corporal presence. The arguments against this novel opinion are developed at great length in the various writings of the Reformation period, and all that can be attempted in the present context is a brief summary.

For one thing, even if we assume that the distinction between substance and accidents is valid, to postulate a change of substance gives rise to almost as many difficulties as it solves. For instance, is it really possible to conceive of one substance in connection with accidents which plainly belong to another? If so, do we not ascribe to God what is almost an act of deception or conjuring? Is it not the case that when God works miracles He works real miracles which may be plainly perceived as such, and not philosophical miracles which are immune from investigation? Even the fact that all things are possible to God is not a real argument, for it does not give us liberty to speculate on all the things that God might do, but merely the confidence to accept the things that He actually wills to do, and has done, and does, as recorded in Holy Scripture. Already, then, from this general standpoint, the doctrine of the real presence of Christ in the Supper is not convincing.

Again, on general grounds, it may be asked whether this particular understanding of the nature of reality is valid and scriptural? Can we make the distinction between substance and accidents intrinsic to this whole view? Whether or not the Reformers were *Nominalists* rather than *Realists* in philosophical training and outlook is not quite the point here. It may well be that some of them inclined in this direction. But what really counts is whether the realism of the Middle Ages is a genuinely biblical realism. Does it not owe more to Greek philosophy than to the Bible? And if this is the case, is it not a serious and radical mistake to suspend a supposed truth of such importance upon so questionable a thesis? Even if we are convinced that some form of corporal presence is demanded by Christ's own statement, we surely go too far if we enforce a dogma of transubstantiation so dependent upon a particular philosophical outlook.

But there are more detailed objections as well, especially in relation to the texts upon which the Romanist teaching is finally based. It is incontestable, of course, that when Christ takes the bread He says: "This is my body," and that when He takes the cup He says: "This is my blood."[6] But there are obvious difficulties in the way of taking this to mean that Christ's body and blood are literally and corporally present in or with or under the bread and wine. First, Christ's body and blood are actually present at the institution in addition to the bread and wine. Hence, while we need not adopt the absurd simplification of Carlstadt that when Christ spoke the words He referred to His own person rather than the bread and wine, it is equally absurd to think that He is confusing the disciples with an unexplained duplication of His presence. Admittedly, this is not impossible on the philosophical assumptions of the doctrine. But it is pointless in any case, and to those unacquainted with this philosophy incomprehensible.

Again, in the context both of the Last Supper and of the discourse in John 6, there can be little doubt that the statements are not meant to be taken in a strictly literal sense.[7] As the Reformers point out, the passover itself contains a similar identification of the bread not only with bread of affliction eaten in Egypt, but even with the event of the passover itself,[8] so that while an identity of substance might be argued in the first case it is plainly impossible in the second. But the Lord's Supper is obviously a sacrament of the true passover of Christ Himself sacrificed for us.[9] And

6. Matt. 26:26, 28, and par.
7. Cf. John 6:63.
8. Exod. 12:24.
9. I Cor. 5:4.

after the feeding of the five thousand, which took place at the time of the passover,[10] we are told that Christ pointed the people away from any corporal eating, whether of accidents or substance, to the true feeding upon the bread of life which is in the Spirit.[11] In these circumstances, we do violence to the general sense of Scripture if we insist that on this one occasion a corporal presence and feeding are necessary and important, in substance if not in accidents.

A third difficulty concerns the actual working of the miracle of transubstantiation in relation to the statement itself. If this change takes place when the priest pronounces the words, at what point does the substance cease to be that of bread (or wine) and become that of the body (or blood) of Christ? In other words, does the doctrine really permit a literal acceptance of the statement? When the statement is analyzed, we see that the miracle cannot be related to the two nouns, for we are too soon if we refer it to the "This" and too late if we keep it back until the "My body." Yet if we link it with the verb "is" we ought really to say "becomes" rather than "is." To say that it must be linked with the whole statement is merely to admit that the equation does not stand up to detailed investigation.

A final point along these lines is that in I Corinthians 11 the equation is rather different in the case of the cup, for it is here described as "the new testament in my blood."[12] But surely we cannot seriously suppose that the substance of the cup is here replaced by that of a testament, as the doctrine of transubstantiation would seem to require. In the following verses Paul obstinately continues to speak of the elements rather than the body and blood of Christ.[13] To be sure, this is not a decisive difficulty to the staunch adherent of the doctrine, for the accidents of bread and wine remain. But Paul might have been a little more precise if he had really known the doctrine or wished to proclaim it.

Another scriptural objection to the whole interpretation is that according to the Bible, and the clear teaching of the creed and the fathers, the body of Christ is now in heaven

10. John 6:4.
11. John 6:63.
12. I Cor. 11:26.
13. I Cor. 11:27.

and will remain there until the second advent.[14] There are, of course, many things that we do not know about the risen body of Christ or the place where Christ now is at the right hand of the Father. But the Bible seems to indicate very clearly that Christ will not be bodily present again until He comes at the last day. In this respect no distinction is made between substance and accidents. We are thus forced back upon equally difficult positions if we wish to maintain the doctrine. We might claim that a distinction is implied between substance and accidents. We might argue that the rather indefinable thing called the substance of Christ's body and blood may be present without bringing down Christ from heaven in the body. Or we might boldly affirm that the sacrament is eschatological in the sense of anticipating the coming again of the Lord. But it is evident that none of these explanations has any foundation in Scripture. As Zwingli in particular used to argue, we fight against plain Scriptures and our own confession of faith if we try to have a bodily presence of Christ in the time between His ascension and return. No amount of subtle philosophizing can evade this undeniable truth.

A further point which has to be taken into account is that if we assume that Christ is substantially present in the bread and wine, then we have to accept the fact that He is received by all those who partake of the elements, and therefore that He may be received by the wicked or hypocritical to their damnation. Now the Reformers do not contest a true presence of Christ in the sacrament. They do not dispute that the sacrament may be received by unbelievers to their hurt.[15] They see clearly enough that the Savior is also the Judge, and that the divine work of grace is itself also the work of judgment. But in their view it is quite monstrous to speak of receiving Christ to condemnation. The whole point about the wicked is that the means of grace are to them a token of perdition because they do not receive Christ Himself crucified for them, but only the sign of His broken body and outpoured blood.[16] The fact that the doctrine of transubstantiation

14. Acts 1:9ff.
15. I Cor. 11:29.
16. *Ibid.*

carries with it such distorted implications is sufficient in itself to expose its falsity.

A final series of objections arises in respect to the actual partaking of the bread and wine, and therefore of the alleged substance of Christ's body and blood. What the doctrine proposes is a kind of refined or concealed cannibalism, and the substance of Christ's body and blood is subjected to the indignity of being caught up into the processes of human digestion, or possibly chewed by rats and mice, or even swept up with the refuse if the elements are accidentally spilled, or perhaps going moldy in some damp and ill-ventilated church. If it is replied that these objections are based on a crass interpretation, it may be pointed out that some care was taken in the Middle Ages to deal with these very points. Fasting communion was enjoined very largely to prevent the admixture of the sacred elements with other food. The cup was denied to the laity because spilled wine could not be so easily gathered as a dropped wafer. The reserved sacrament was kept under cover partly to preserve it from marauding animals or rodents. To be sure, this type of difficulty is not the primary reason for dismissing the whole notion. But the fact remains that the doctrine gives rise to these difficulties, too, and that they are not to be evaded by mere protestations of crude misunderstanding.

But if the doctrine of transubstantiation cannot be accepted, the question arises what is meant by the statement of Christ that the bread and wine are His body and blood, and in what sense He may rightly be said and known to be present in the sacrament. The two questions come to very much the same thing, for it is only in virtue of Christ's statement that the question of His presence becomes a particular issue in relation to the Supper. We may thus begin by considering the Reformers' interpretation of the saying, and then review the implications of this interpretation in relation to the presence.

On the question of interpretation, there is of course a serious divergence, for Luther and his followers argue that the saying must in some way be taken at its face value and given a literal sense. It is this which gives rise to the subtleties of consubstantiation on the one side and the oversimplification of Carlstadt on the other. But the majority of the

Reformers agree that the statement cannot be construed as a strict equation, but must be taken to mean that the bread signifies, represents, or stands for the body, and the wine for the blood. In other words, it is a meaningful and effective sign, according to the general sense and purpose of a sacrament.

In favor of this view, the following consideration may be advanced. In the first place, there are similar sayings (e.g., "I am the door") [17] in which a literal interpretation is clearly excluded. Second, it is in keeping with the general usage of the Bible that sign and thing signified should be brought into close juxtaposition, but without literal equation or confusion.[18] Third, the Bible makes it plain that the elements of bread and wine remain,[19] and knows nothing of the philosophical attempts to explain how they can both be and not be bread and wine at the same time. Fourth, it is obvious that the fathers adopted a similar line of understanding.

But does this mean that in the bread and wine, or in the sacramental action, we have only signs of the incarnate Christ and His saving work? This is the objection of the traditionalists who feel that the Reformed understanding gives us no more than a bare symbolism in which the sacrament becomes simply a memorial feast. It is also the complaint of Luther who believes that the starkness of the saying of Christ forces us to something more vivid and profound. And there can be no doubt that many Protestants, like the 16th century Anabaptists, do in fact regard the elements as no more than an empty sign.

The main Reformers, however, refuse to be driven into the false alternative of a substantial presence or no presence at all. As Ridley claimed in answer to the representatives of transubstantiation, the true doctrine is that while we cannot speak of the "real" presence in the technical sense, in the more general sense Christ is really present in this sacrament as in all the means of grace. And in virtue of the closeness of the sign to His death and passion, the reality of His saving presence is perhaps brought home to us more vividly and

17. John 10:9.
18. As in the case of the passover.
19. I Cor. 11.24.

concretely in this sign than in baptism or even verbal proclamation. But in what sense and to what extent?

First, He is naturally present according to His deity, as the eternal Logos.[20] In all these matters we have to do with God. There can thus be no question of a mere memorial, as though we were simply celebrating the great action of a great man. The One whose death we commemorate is the Creator and Lord of all things, present always and in all things, and therefore not to be disregarded in these elements which speak particularly of His incarnate work.

But if this were all, it might be argued that Christ is equally present in everything which is done, and therefore the sacrament has no special value or significance as a means of grace. It has thus to be added, secondly, that in the sacrament we have to reckon with the presence of Christ incarnate, crucified, risen, and ascended. The action is the sacrament of what Christ did in the flesh,[21] for us men and for our salvation; and it is therefore with the true presence of the incarnate Christ that we have to do when we partake of the elements.

Properly to understand the relationship between Christ and the elements, we have to see in the sacrament a reflection of the incarnation itself. On the one hand, we have the human side, the bread and wine; and these are not destroyed, subsumed, or changed, but remain in their natural substance. On the other hand, however, we have the divine, or divine-human side, the incarnate Christ Himself; and He, too, is not changed into the elements or confused with them, but remains in His natural substance. Luther was quite right to see a close connection between the sacrament and the incarnation. But he fell into the same error as the medieval theologians and tried to have a substantial unity. The Anabaptists on the other side divorced the two sides of the word and sacrament too harshly, not seeing the real connection between the two. In a true interpretation, we see that in this action, as in baptism and preaching, we have to do with two things which can neither be confused nor divided, Christ Himself being truly present as bread and wine are taken, blessed, and distributed.

20. John 1:1ff.
21. John 1:14.

This presence of Christ is, of course, a presence in the
Holy Spirit. It is not the presence of Christ as in His earthly
ministry nor His final triumph. He Himself comes according
to His promise, but He comes by the Holy Ghost whom He
has sent.[22] It is thus a "spiritual" presence, not in the vague
sense in which we think of this today, but in the concrete
and specific sense of a true presence mediated by the Spirit.
The Spirit is the One who in word and sacrament presents
Christ to us in this time between His coming and His coming
again. It is the error of transubstantiation on the one side
to by-pass the work of the Holy Spirit, i.e., to try to have
Christ without the Spirit, and of the Anabaptists on the
other to rationalize or "spiritualize" it, i.e., to try to have
the Spirit without Christ. But neither course is possible. The
Spirit is genuinely the Spirit of Christ, and therefore there
can be no presence of Christ without the Spirit, and no Spirit
without the presence of Christ.

The Holy Spirit mediates the presence of Christ in a two-
fold way. In the first place, He makes Christ present to us,
so that as we take the bread and wine we are genuinely in
the presence of the One who took flesh and gave His body
and blood and was raised again for us.[23] There is no question
here of re-presenting Christ, either before men or before
God. It is a question of making Him present, making Him
our contemporary, so that the historical difficulty seen by
Lessing is met and overcome. But, secondly, we ourselves
are lifted up into the presence of the Christ who lived and
died and rose and ascended for us. Our affections are thus
called from earthly things[24] and we are set in the upward
movement with Christ which is the gracious consequence of
His downward movement for us. These two aspects are not
really contradictory, but complementary. It is as Christ
comes down for us that we are raised with Him. And we are
raised with Him because, coming down for us, He has made
Himself one with us, and our true life is that which is hid
with Christ in God.

But is this an objective presence, or is it something which
may be expected only when certain conditions are fulfilled on

22. John 14:18, 16:4.
23. John 16:14.
24. Col. 3:1ff.

the part of the communicant? At this point we must be careful not to fall into the subjectivism which is a constant threat to sacramental teaching. When the sacraments are duly administered, and the word proclaimed, Christ is always present by the Spirit, and His gifts of grace are proffered to all those who come. In this sense we may rightly speak of an objective presence of Christ. Neither fear of a doctrine of automatic efficacy nor the experience of those who do not consciously realize this presence must be allowed to jostle us away from this true Reformation insight.

On the other hand, not all those who partake of the elements necessarily perceive Christ or receive His gracious benefits. As it is by the Holy Spirit that Christ is present, so it is by the Holy Spirit that His presence is known and His grace received. But the movement of the Holy Spirit in the true recipient is that of repentance and faith; and therefore it is only in genuine repentance and faith that the presence of Christ is perceived and His benefits are appropriated. As it is with the Lord Himself in His earthly life, or with the word which speaks of Him, so it is with the sacrament which attests Him. Jesus is always the Christ, but not all who meet with Him know Him as He really is; only faith can pierce the veil. His word is always the word of life and truth, but not all who read or hear it receive it as the word of the living God. Similarly, Christ is always present in the sacrament, but only those who receive in faith may know His presence to their soul's profit. The unbeliever eats and drinks damnation to himself, as the medieval church had rightly said. But this is not because he eats and drinks Christ. It is for the very opposite reason — that He does not discern the Lord's body and therefore does not receive Christ and His salvation.[25] Faith alone is the stretched out hand by which Christ Himself is received, as the physical hand is stretched out to receive the elements.

But to insist upon the necessity of faith for a perception of the presence is not to call merely for a subjective experience, as though this were a necessary condition of the effective grace of the sacrament. For faith itself, the faith which receives and therefore saves, is the gift of the Holy Ghost.[26]

25. I Cor. 11:29.
26. Eph. 2:8.

In Holy Communion, therefore, as in baptism and all our dealings with Jesus Christ, we must come with prayer that the Holy Spirit will do His work, giving us grace to perceive the Christ who is present whether we know it or not, and thus to believe in Him, and to receive the sacrament to our profit and strengthening. When we do this, we come in faith, denying ourselves and casting ourselves upon God. And whether or not we have any conscious experience, we know what it means when the Bible says that faith is added to faith, and that to him that hath it shall be given.[27] For the sacrament is to us a means of grace and not a sign of condemnation. It brings before us the saving work of Christ. It lifts us up to our ascended Lord. It sets us before the Savior Himself, present by the Holy Ghost.

27. Matt. 25:29.

CHAPTER EIGHT

THE EUCHARISTIC SACRIFICE

CLOSELY LINKED with the medieval doctrine of the presence of Christ is that of the so-called sacrifice of the mass. It has always been seen that the Lord's Supper stands in a particularly close connection to the death and passion of Christ. The very circumstances of its institution, the nature of the sign, and the references of the Lord both to His offered body and blood and also to the cup which He had to drink — all these make it inevitable and right that this connection should be seen and emphasized. But the doctrine of the substantial presence of Christ's body and blood in the sacrament gives to this necessary connection a new and unfortunate twist. For if the body and blood of Christ are substantially present, then may it not be argued that in some sense they are offered again in the eucharistic action? This is the conclusion which is drawn and elaborated in the understanding of the mass as a sacrifice.

A precarious basis for the conclusion is found in the Bible itself. The basis is again to be found in Christ's saying at the institution. Linguistic evidence is adduced to show that in certain cases the word normally rendered "Do this," can bear the sense of "Offer this."[1] Christ's command is thus construed as the institution of a new and bloodless sacrifice. This is linked up with various other allusions in the Old and New Testaments, such as the pure offering of Malachi 1[2] and the altar of Hebrews 13;[3] and scriptural justification is thought to be found for the doctrine.

1. Luke 22:19.
2. Mal. 1:11.
3. Heb. 13:10.

Briefly, the action is understood as follows. When the mass is celebrated, the miracle of transubstantiation takes place at some point in the consecration. The accidents of bread and wine remain, but the substance is now that of the body and blood of Christ. Under the accidents of bread and wine, this substance is now immolated in the eucharistic action, and an offering is thus made for sin. This offering rather than communion is the primary meaning and purpose of the sacrament; and in virtue of this sacrifice the table is properly an altar and the minister is ordained not merely a presbyter but a sacrificing priest, and decked out with all the trappings of his office.

But the question arises, what is the point of this continual offering when we are told by the Bible that there is one offering for sins forever?[4] It is here that we can see the full seriousness of the sacramentalist misunderstanding of baptism to which reference has already been made in Chapter Four. To be sure, there is no intention of denying the uniqueness or fullness of Christ's sacrifice on Calvary. This is the only ground of our eternal salvation. Not only are the baptized washed in virtue of this sacrifice, but if they fall into mortal sin they can escape hell only as they seek refuge in this work by the way of penance. Yet while the sacrifice of Christ is the only ground of eternal remission, there are certain temporal penalties of mortal and venial sin after baptism which do not come under the scope of this eternal work. And while these penalties do not carry with them the terror of perdition, they are serious enough for us to seek ways of mitigation, and for a merciful God to provide us with such ways. Among such ways, one of the most potent is the sacrifice of the mass.

It is one of the most potent for the following reasons. First, it was instituted by the Lord Himself. Second, it involves His own substantial presence. Third, it is a clear reflection and lesser repetition of the offering of Calvary. Fourth, it can be repeated *ad infinitum*. Fifth, its efficacy is not restricted to those present at its celebration. And finally, it avails no less for the dead than for the living. In these circumstances, it is hardly surprising that this so-called offering is the focus of all Roman Catholic worship, piety, and

4. Heb. 9:28.

religious life, and a most lucrative source of income through the endowment of masses for the dead.

The attack upon the sacrifice of the mass gathers together many of the most important Reformation objections to the whole medieval system and thus occupies a central place in the work of doctrinal reform. Most of the points in question have already been treated in other connections, and we may therefore content ourselves with a brief summary which will bring out their relevance to the present topic.

For one thing, the Reformers cannot accept that there is a substantial presence of Christ, and therefore the whole basis of the doctrine is undermined. Christ cannot be offered again unless He is actually there in the elements. Once this foundation is removed, the rest of the structure comes crashing to the ground.

Again, the Reformers do not agree that there is any scriptural evidence for the doctrine. The natural rendering of the "Do this" in Christ's saying is that the disciples should repeat His own action in the taking, blessing and distributing of bread and wine; and this is made clear by the words "in remembrance of me,"[5] which bring out the point of the action. The prophecy in Malachi, if it refers to a sacrifice of the church, may plainly be connected with our sacrifice either of praise and thanksgiving or of ourselves, and in the verse in Hebrews it may well be that the reference is to the Old Testament altar. In any case, the Bible does not provide any warrant for regarding the sacrament as a sacrifice.

Again, for all the attempted safeguards and distinctions, the doctrine is quite incompatible with the uniqueness of Christ's self-offering on the cross. In medieval practice, the pains of purgatory are far more important that those of hell, which may normally be escaped with very little difficulty. The sacrifice of Christ is thus an indispensable basis, but like baptism it is of little practical relevance. What matters is that there should be escape from more pressing dangers which the sacrifice of Christ is unable to overcome. The Bible itself, however, drives us back again and again to the one sacrifice for sins forever, to the one Mediator who is both priest and victim; and it does so with no reservations or

5. Luke 22:19.

distinctions. A concern for this basic truth demands that the sacrifice of the mass should be rejected.

Again, the Reformers see that the whole idea of temporal penalties, especially in purgatory, is quite unfounded. That there are certain consequences of sin in this life cannot be denied. But we have no warrant at all for believing either that these consequences can be mitigated by any actions or that there are undefined consequences in an intermediate state which can be relieved by priestly action. This view is not only without foundation in the Bible but is based upon a complete misunderstanding of the substitutionary work of Christ, of the nature of the Christian life of faith, and of what is meant by eternal salvation. But without these temporal penalties, there is no point in the so-called sacrifices, and therefore on this count again the doctrine falls to the ground.

Finally, it is seen that this insistence upon an offering of the mass shifts the balance of the sacrament. It points us away from the true center, which is the one offering of Christ in His death and passion. It gives a false importance to the minister, who with his power to summon and offer Christ becomes in a limited sphere the mediator between God and the people. It sets the action in an alien setting tricked out with features borrowed from paganism or from the fulfilled and therefore superseded ritual of the Old Testament. And it so destroys the meaning of the sacrament as a communion that participation is of little importance, and masses may even be celebrated without a congregation at all.

In their concern to refute this erroneous doctrine, the Reformers do not, of course, fall into the mistake of isolating the sacrament from the whole conception of sacrifice. As we have seen in our assessment of the Reformation understanding, there is a genuine sense in which the Lord's Supper must be understood sacrificially. But care must be taken to see that this is not stated in the wrong way, especially when we consider the relationship of the sacrament to the crucifixion. Even within Protestantism there have been ways of stating the relationship which have approximated the Roman Catholic teaching, although without the basis in transubstantiation or the idea of a literal immolation and atonement for the temporal penalties of sin.

Perhaps the most widespread and attractive of these is the notion of a re-presentation of the offering of Calvary. This is Protestant as opposed to Roman Catholic in many important respects. It builds on the contention of the Reformers that the "is" of Christ's statement is to be taken in the sense of "represents." It does not contend for a substantial presence of Christ and therefore for a real immolation. It is thus careful not to derogate from the honor of the one sacrifice of Christ. And it links up with a conception which is often found in Evangelical circles — that of pleading the merits of Christ and the efficacy of His work. For the point is that in the administration of the Supper we set forth Christ in His death and passion, not merely before the people, but before God the Father, offering Him again in the bread and wine, and thus securing our access to the Father and strengthening our faith in His saving work. In this view, it is right enough to think of Holy Communion as an offering (in the sense of a re-presentation), and therefore we may describe the table as an altar and the minister as a quasi-mediatorial priest, giving to the whole service a sacrificial slant and setting.

Now there is no point in confusing this reinterpretation with the clear-cut Roman Catholic doctrine. It is indefinite enough to allow some of those who profess it to be medievalists at heart; but there can be no doubt that in the minds of others it is intended in a non-medieval and even Evangelical sense. Yet, even on the most favorable understanding, it is not a view which is compatible with the true insight of the Reformation. From the standpoint of Reformation teaching the following objections may be raised against it.

First, we have no biblical authority for the concept of re-presentation in the sense of a secondary offering which reflects and pleads the sacrifice of Calvary. There is a very real sense in which the bread and wine taken, blessed, and distributed bear witness to this sacrifice, shewing forth the Lord's death.[6] But there is no suggestion, even in a secondary or derivative sense, of the sacrament being itself an offering. Indeed, the fact that no blood-shedding is involved in the action makes it plain that from a scriptural standpoint the whole idea of immolation is deliberately excluded. An action is chosen which obviously corresponds to the giving of

6. I Cor. 11:26.

Christ's body and blood, but equally obviously does not in any sense or to any extent repeat it. Now that the blood of Christ has been once shed for sin, there is no need either for a fresh sacrifice or for the re-presentation of this one offering.

Second, the orientation of the interpretation seems to be wrong, for the primary purpose of sacraments is not to remind God of the saving work of Christ, but to attest it to us. If there is a true sense in which the minister may be regarded as a mediator in his dispensing of word and sacrament, it is as the representative of Christ holding out in speech and action the reconciling word. Even here it is better to avoid the term *mediator,* for the Bible tells us plainly that there is one Mediator between God and man.[7] In any case, however, it is a mistake to think of the sacrament as a preaching of the Gospel to God in order that on the basis of the work which He Himself has done He may be favorable to the people. The sacrament does not consist primarily in intercession, although it must certainly be carried through in prayer, and in an attitude of prayer. It is part of the ministry of proclamation, addressed to man and not to God. If the death of the Lord is shown forth, it is to believers and to the world.

Third, we have no reason to link up the sacrament either with the intercessory work of Christ or with His eternal self-offering. It is true that as the One who died and rose again for us, Christ is now our Advocate in heaven.[8] It is also true that that which was once done in history on the cross has an eternal background.[9] But the sacrament is neither a part of the intercessory work of Christ on the one side, nor a necessary or possible re-presentation of the eternal offering on the other. It tells us that Christ is our Advocate, and therefore invites us to put our trust in Him, to rest in His saving efficacy. But it is not itself a part of the advocacy. It tells us that what happened on Golgotha happened in fulfillment of God's reconciling purpose from eternity, and therefore summons us to the complementary movement of penitence and faith. But it is not another historical concretion of this eternal offering. If there is pleading of Christ

7. I Tim. 2:5.
8. I John 2:1.
9. I Pet. 1:20.

and His merits, it is in response to the sacramental action which sets Christ and His merits before us, not in the action itself.

The point as the Reformers see it is quite simply that the sacrament is connected with the one sacrifice of Calvary as proclamation, as a visible and tangible word of the cross. This is the plain but powerful truth which underlies the distortions of medieval doctrine on the one hand and the subtle misinterpretation of some forms of Protestantism on the other. In obedience to the Lord's command, we take the bread and wine which are to us His body and blood. We break and outpour them in eloquent proclamation of the fact that He gave His body and blood both in life and death. And we take them in thankful acknowledgment that He did so in our place and on our behalf.

Does this mean that the sacrament is a mere symbol of sacrifice, an analogous action which sets us in mind of the cross? From the human standpoint, this is true; although we do well not to give the word *mere* a derogatory sense, as though it were only a little thing to have this eloquent sign of the cross. But, as we have seen, there is more than a human side, for the means of grace are not merely human devices but potent instruments in the hands of the Holy Spirit. Undertaken in prayer and applied by the Spirit, the sacrament is not a mere reminder of the sacrifice which took place on Calvary, but a means to make that one sacrifice present to us, to give it contemporaneity with us or *vice versa,* to bring vividly and concretely before us what it was that our incarnate, crucified, and risen Lord did, and that He did it for us. In other words, the eucharistic offering is not a secondary repetition which procures certain less essential but helpful benefits. Nor is it a derivative re-presentation. It is the one offering itself, which is the true cup as it is the true baptism.[10] And it is this offering attested and shown us by the human action, but also set before us by the Holy Spirit, so that spiritually, i.e., in the Spirit, Christ Himself is present in the self-offering of His death, and we thankfully identify ourselves with Him.

But again, to say that the sacrament is used by the Holy Spirit to bring the one sacrifice of Calvary before us, or to

10. Matt. 26:39.

set us in the presence of that one sacrifice, is to say that it must be received in penitence and faith and therefore in gratitude. The inward work of the Holy Spirit is faith. It is with the eyes of faith that we see Christ Himself, and are set before His one self-offering for us. It is with the hand of faith that we receive His benefits. It is faith which reposes upon the finished work of Christ, and is thus strengthened by the representation of that work. To those who do not believe, or are not prepared to believe, the sacrament may well be the mere recollection of an historical event, with no particular meaning or relevance. Indeed, it may be no more than a religious observance. For the true reality is not perceived. But when we come with faith, or with a readiness for faith, the Holy Spirit takes us beyond the human sign to the thing signified, to the cross itself where the sacrificial obedience of the Son found its fulfillment in the self-offering of death, and in this sense and to this extent, in the Holy Spirit and to faith, the sacrament is the sacrifice, and faith is confirmed and strengthened. True faith does not credulously accept the imagined philosophical miracle of transubstantiation, and thus cling to the secondary sacrifice of Christ's body and blood in the mass. It brings us into the presence of Christ Himself by the Spirit, and therefore to the supreme and once-for-all sacrifice of Calvary, in which it may confidently repose both in this world and to all eternity for the forgiveness of all sin.

It is on the basis of this perception of the one sacrifice of Christ that the Lord's Supper is the responsive sacrifice of praise and thanksgiving. Gratitude is the right answer to the grace of God. When we see what God has done, vividly brought before us by the Holy Spirit, we pour out our hearts in thankfulness to God, knowing that for Christ's sake He will graciously accept that which we are quite unworthy to offer. This aspect has already been mentioned in our survey of the positive teaching of the Reformers, and we need not labor it here. But it is worth emphasizing that this is no little thing that we are permitted to offer, as though the offering of praise and thanksgiving were ordinary and unimportant compared with the supposed mediatorial sacrifice of the mass. In the Bible it is only wicked men who are allowed to lay violent hands on the Son of God, delivering Him up in fulfillment of His own gracious self-delivering.[11] We do ourselves little credit by trying to repeat the action of Judas, Caiaphas, Herod, and Pilate. But the offering which God does require and approve, and which is therefore our supreme mystery and glory as Christians, is that of our gratitude and adoration. This is something which we shall be privileged to offer into eternity itself.[12] In face of the fullness of Christ's own sacrifice for us, we do well to realize that this high sacrifice of praise is also required of us, and to make the sacrament a genuine eucharist, an occasion of humble but victorious thankfulness and joy.

And praise, as we have seen, includes not merely the offering of the heart and lips, but also of the life and activity.[13] If Christ has taken our place, we can accept our death and resurrection in Him. We can genuinely deny ourselves, reckoning ourselves dead to the old past. We can genuinely live the new life which is Christ in us and for us, yielding all our powers and opportunities to His direction and service. Here again, we must not minimize the sacrifice which we are permitted. To try to offer even a derivative sacrifice for sin is to be guilty of the very pride and folly which harried Christ to His death, but from which He died to free us. It is no glory to us to offer up Christ to death, even under the accidents of bread and wine. Only sinners can ever desire to do such a thing, and in their sinful hands the offering up of Christ is a wicked assault upon their Brother, King and God. God alone can offer up Himself for us, and this He has done once and for all upon the cross. What we can do as believers is to respond to His self-offering by offering ourselves to Him, making Him our own, receiving Him in that action of penitence, faith, and obedience which means our corresponding death and resurrection with Christ. This self-dedication is the true answer in the Spirit to the one sacrifice of Christ presented to faith when the bread and wine are taken and distributed.

In conclusion, it is to be stressed that the response itself, the sacrifice of praise and service, is a work of the Holy Spirit. The great error of false doctrines of the eucharistic

11. Acts 2:23.
12. Eph. 1:12, 2:4.
13. I Pet. 2:9.

sacrifice is that they ignore or misunderstand the work of the Holy Ghost. They either try to go straight to Christ Himself, or they try to force the Holy Spirit to do something other than what which He has come to do. But even in the Reformation understanding, there is a danger of leaving out the Holy Spirit. We can begin to talk of spiritual sacrifices as though we meant only something intellectual or emotional, a subjective response in us. We must always remember that our praise and dedication are a spiritual offering in the strict sense of a response in the Spirit. As it is through the Spirit that Christ offered Himself,[14] and His sacrifice is made present to us, so it is in the Spirit that we can make the appropriate answer of thanksgiving and service.[15] Here again, as in baptism and our reading and hearing of the word, we must pray always for the Holy Ghost, that He may not only show us the things of Jesus, but may move our inward beings to the responsive penitence and faith. The Holy Spirit Himself is the ultimate Witness and Worker, and therefore we must always pray in our hearts: *Veni Creator Spiritus.*

14. Heb. 9:14.
15. Rom. 8:1ff.

CONCLUSION

WE HAVE NOW CONCLUDED our brief survey of the sacraments as they are understood by the Reformation churches. It cannot be pretended, of course, that a full account has been given. The Reformers themselves gave to both sacraments, and to the whole theme of sacramental theology, a good deal of detailed attention. But the main lines of interpretation have been given, and the Reformation understanding marked off from medieval errors on the one side and more modern misunderstanding on the other. It now remains simply to drive home two points which have already been mentioned in the Introduction.

In the first place, it must be understood that Reformation doctrine is always subject to the supreme test of Holy Scripture, and cannot therefore be irreformable in the sense of Romanist dogma. Dogmaticians of the Reformation churches are always pleased to refer back to the first Reformers and the great confessions, and they must always admit with astonishment the great knowledge which these fathers had of the Bible, and their remarkable insight into biblical truth. There can be no easy departing from their presentation of sacramental or any other doctrine. Yet the Reformers and their confessions cannot be made a fetter to bind the church, preventing it from a free hearing and following of the word of God. We must always be ready to receive from the Holy Spirit new or better understanding, so long as it is genuinely from the Bible itself. In the present study we have seen little cause to dissent from the Reformation fathers; but it is of the very essence of their own approach that we should be prepared to do so, to correct, amend, or re-state their teaching, if ever our study of the Bible should lead us in this direction. A mark of genuine Reformation teaching is that is it not fixed or static, but always reformable under the word of God.

Secondly, the sacraments have been given us, not merely that we should study and assess and understand them, but

primarily and supremely that we should use them. This does
not mean that understanding is unimportant. A false view of
the sacraments can be a hindrance to their proper use and
therefore to their effective operation. To know their meaning
and purpose is to be helped to their true enjoyment. But
even the theologian cannot treat them merely as a theme of
academic study. He cannot think that his own work in relation to them is of primary or autonomous value. He realizes
that the Holy Spirit is not merely a Spirit of the intellect, so
that even with a false doctrine of the sacraments, they may
be genuine means of grace, and even with the most correct
understanding, they may be robbed of their real value. The
one necessary thing about the sacraments is to use them, to
be baptized and to take the bread and wine in fulfillment of
the Lord's command.

But properly to use them, as we have seen, is to do so with
a readiness to see Christ Himself and His saving work, and
therefore with prayer to the Holy Spirit that He may dispose
of the means which He Himself has chosen and of which He
Himself is the Lord. Whatever else we may do or not do,
however great or little may be our understanding, always
and in all circumstances we must be prepared to use the
means which God has seen fit to give us, and in the spirit of
humble devotion to expect and to receive the grace which He
is more than ready to give. If we will do this, our knowledge
of the grace and operation of the sacraments will always
exceed even our best attempts at understanding; and we
shall continually give thanks to God that for all our ignorance
and obstinacy He deals with us more graciously in word and
sacrament than we either desire or deserve.

GENERAL INDEX

Anabaptists, 28, 35, 51-55, 90, 91, 92

Anglican Church, see Church of England

Augustine, 17, 80

Baptism
administration of, 24, 27, 28, 34-43
adult, 39, 40, 56
and Christian unity, 28
and the Gospel, 13-19, 40, 45, 54
and our resurrection, 27
and suffering and death, 26-27
consecration of water, 35-36
definition of, 20
errors and problems regarding, 42-57
formula for, 37
indiscriminate practice of, 41-42
infant, 35, 40, 41, 47, 53-54, 56, 57
meaning of, 21-33
minister of, 39-40, 42
mode of application, 35
origin of, 20
private, 38-40
recipients of, 35, 40, 60
relation to God, the Father, 15-19, 21-23, 46, 51
relation to the Holy Spirit, 15-19, 21-23, 30, 31, 33, 40, 45, 46, 51
relation to Jesus Christ, 12-13, 15-19, 21-23, 46-52, 54, 56
response to, 23-26, 30-33, 56
sin after, 48-51, 96, 98
subjectivization of, 44-57, 60
threefold, 36
water, 34, 35

Bible, biblical, 11, 12, 15, 16, 18, 34, 35, 36, 37, 38, 51, 52, 55, 56, 64, 70, 71, 72, 77, 85, 86, 87, 88, 90, 94, 95, 96, 97, 98, 99, 100

Caiaphas, 103

Carlstadt, 86, 89

Church Fathers, 35, 87, 90

Church of England, 35, 36, 37, 38, 39, 41, 48, 66, 71, 74, 75, 76, 78, 79

Circumcision, 14, 40, 53, 56

Confirmation, 13, 14, 75

Cornelius, 18, 53

Cranmer, 36, 82

Denominationalism, 64, 65

Evangelicalism, 55, 57, 99

Herod, 103

John the apostle, 80

John the Baptist 20, 53

Jud, 36

Judas, 80, 103

Kant, 55

Lessing, 92

Liberalism, Protestant, 54, 55; Romantic, 51

Lord's Supper
administration of, 70-81
adoration of elements in, 72
and church unity, 64, 65
and eschatological hope, 68-69
and fellowship, 61-64
and Gospel, 13-19, 67
and offertory, 66, 67, 77-78
and preaching, 77
as sacrifice, 95-104
bread and wine, 67, 70, 71, 79, 83, 84, 86, 87, 89, 90, 91, 96, 97, 99, 101, 103

SCRIPTURE INDEX

109

9 780802 863300

Made in the USA
Lexington, KY
15 December 2016